CW01207896

Talbot Mundy

The Mystery of Khufu's Tomb
(Unabridged)

OK Publishing 2021

Talbot Mundy
The Mystery of Khufu's Tomb

(Unabridged)

Published by
MUSAICUM
Books

- Advanced Digital Solutions & High-Quality book Formatting -

musaicumbooks@okpublishing.info

2021 OK Publishing

ISBN 978-80-272-7950-0

Contents

CHAPTER I Which is a kind of preface	11
CHAPTER II Moustapha Pasha	15
CHAPTER III "You talk like the British government"	19
CHAPTER IV Zoom of the Zee-Bar-Zee	23
CHAPTER V Zezwinski of the Zee-Bar-Zee	29
CHAPTER VI "A land in which death is not difficult, but life has its complexities"	35
CHAPTER VII "The answer is still no"—"Then go to the Devil!"	41
CHAPTER VIII "If you want to bet I'll bet with you"	43
CHAPTER IX "Lent us by Ah Li Wan"	48
CHAPTER X "Whom Allah hath made mad let none offend"	53
CHAPTER XI "Too much water!"	60
CHAPTER XII "Damn-fool thinkee money good for dead man. Makee plenty more mistake"	65
CHAPTER XIII "Go to it, boys!"	71
CHAPTER XIV "Please come quickly!"	76
CHAPTER XV "Speak, o man of swift decisions!"	84
CHAPTER XVI "Cleopatra, who would have liked to sell Egypt's soul again"	87
CHAPTER XVII Magnificent simplicity	92

CHAPTER I
Which is a kind of preface

We Americans are ostriches. We stick well meaning heads into the political sands of these United States, swear-probably correctly-they are better than all other sands, and accordingly declare ourselves free for ever from entangling alliances. "Struthio camelus," whose plumes are plucked for market while his head, stowed snugly in a stocking, "sees no evil, hears no evil, speaks no evil," and who then struts about asserting that a plucked and smarting rump is fashionable, ought to be our national bird, not the all-seeing eagle.

But this isn't an effort to reform the United States. We're the finest there is or ever was, only rather more entangled with the old world than we think.

The Great Pyramid of Gizeh is older than the Declaration of Independence, and its claims continue to have precedence, our elected statesmen notwithstanding. Statesmen understand not much beyond the drift of popular opinion; but conspirators have always understood that the safest place to conspire in is the centre of the establishment they aim at.

The men whose lives are spent mainly in the open are the widest awake. To assert the contrary is only another phase of the ostrich habit. If a man wipes his knife on the seat of his trousers and knows where the cinnamon bear will be rooting at six a.m., he's not necessarily less enlightened than the fellow who thinks he knows what the editorials in the morning paper really mean. That partly explains why the best policemen come from the plough-tail and the woods, and cities don't often produce Abe Lincolns.

All this sounds rather far from Egypt and the Pyramid of Gizeh, but is not. Few people know or knew why the Great Pyramid was built. Hundreds of thousands toiled at the making of it, most of whom thought they knew, just as most of the people who take the subway in the morning think they know why, and are deluded. They believed what they were told. They were told what was considered good for them to think. The men who told them knew hardly any more but were getting a profit, and hard cash always did look like Euclid's Q.E.D. But the men who really did know why the Pyramid was building held their tongues and toiled elsewhere, also for cash, except Khufu himself, who was the arch-type of perfect profiteers.

Khufu was king of Upper and Lower Egypt in those days. Cash dividends did not trouble him much, for he had the taxes to draw on and auditors passed his vouchers without comment. Consequently the man in the street of to-day might be paying higher taxes on account of old Khufu, if Joan Angela Leich hadn't just contrived to miss me with her Ford one dark night on the Geiger Trail; which sounds incredible.

But so is Joan Angela incredible; I'm coming to her presently. Everybody knows her who isn't fenced in by apartment-house blocks. If she had pushed me over the edge of the Geiger that night, you, who read this, would be paying for more armaments.

But it was Khufu who started the trouble. He is better known to fame as Cheops, and we know pretty well what he looked like.

He was a calm, proud, confident-appearing man, with an obvious sense of his own importance and a smile that seemed to say: "Carry on, boys. What's good for me is good for you," Being city folk, he had them all in one place where they had got to listen. Spell-binders laid the argument on thick in one direction; in the other the overseers laid on the lash; and the minstrels, who were the equivalent of the daily Press in those days, praised all concerned.

But right here I'm going to be called in question by the Egyptologists unless I hasten to explain. It will be said with a certain amount of surface truth that the Egyptians who laboured at building the Pyramid were peasants on vacation. Work ceased in the fields when the Nile had overflowed, and they were kept out of mischief by thoughtful superiors, who provided wholesome amusement with educational value that incidentally promoted trade. When the Nile receded at the end of three months, those who had survived the education were permitted to return home and go to work in the fields again, in order to raise crops, with which to pay the taxes, that should keep the ball a-rolling and Jack Pharaoh's pyramid a-building again next season. That is what the text-book writers will assert.

But those peasants were city folk. Egypt was always one great straggling city, with one wide avenue-the Nile-running straight down the middle of it. Everybody lived on Main Street, and they all do still; there was, and is, nowhere else to live, and if the Nile were to dry up Egypt would disappear.

Living on one long street, Egyptians all look alike, think alike, and react to the same inducement. You can't change the Nile, but it will change you, and if you stay there long enough will pattern you until you resemble all the others. Egypt has been invaded scores of times, overrun, looted, conquered, and made to pay tribute; its women have been forced to intermarry with the conquerors, because they are beautiful women with the eyes of gazelles and with a properly respectful attitude toward the male; so the pure-blooded Egyptian no longer exists. Nevertheless, the Egyptian of to-day is exactly like the Egyptian of four thousand years ago, and so is Egypt, except that nowadays you see blue cotton dungarees in place of unbleached linen; a corrupt style of near-French architecture; and two streets instead of one, since the foreigner built the railway.

Then, just as now, there was always a small crowd of foreigners running things, while the native Egyptian did the work. It was a foreigner who suggested the Great Pyramid to Pharaoh, and who doubtless drafted the design and got the contract. No Egyptian ever lived who was capable of designing it. Khufu provided the money and labour, but there is always someone pulling strings behind the autocrat.

In a later Pharaoh's day another foreigner, Joseph by name, thought of cornering corn. Still another foreigner, Lesseps by name, conceived the Suez Canal and put that through. Only the dirt was shifted by Egyptians because they are Egyptians, and the dividends go elsewhere for the same reason.

You can't change Egypt. Not even its religion has changed except on the surface. The religion of the educated classes century by century may be the nominal creed of the labourer, but it has never got under his skin. He was always a fatalist, always a believer in brute force, born, bred, beaten and buried on the Nile, and tributary to it all his days; and if you want to start trouble on the Nile now you can do it exactly as it was done in Pharaoh's time.

Pharaoh's religion was more than perfunctory, or he would never have run the prodigious political risk of forcing gangs of a hundred thousand men to labour in three-month tricks for thirty year. The priests put him up to it, of course. Pharaoh believed that his future in the next world depended wholly on the amount of material preparation that he made for it in this.

He was not only an arch-profiteer. He pyramided profits. He conceived the idea-or priests conceived it for him-of taking the next world by storm. He would be a king for all eternity. He would outdo all the aristocracy who had had themselves entombed in opulence for generations past.

The peasantry-the real Egyptians, that is, who lived on Main Street and paid taxes or were whipped-were no more impressed by that theory than they are by the Sermon on the Mount to-day. They had a more pragmatic, Nile-mud point of view. They wondered, just as they do to-day if anyone propounds a theory to them, whether there was money in it. It was obvious to them that there was. There was their money in it. Every Pharaoh, and every high official who got buried, had as much of the tax money as he could scrape out of the treasury buried with him for his use in the next world. The dwellers on Main Street, preferring this world to the next, and having toiled in the sun for twelve hours a day to earn that money, did some good, plain, Nile-mud thinking; and the result was what you might expect.

It can't have been long before the insurance Companies, if there were any, who underwrote burglary risks on mausoleums went out of business. It got so that a Pharaoh's mummy was hardly set stiff before the boys were out with pickaxes to break the door down and get the treasure out of the vault. It was no use putting a guard before the door, because you can always bribe the guard in Egypt, anyhow, and the guard, being peasants in uniform would be quite as anxious to get their share of the loot as anybody else. No doubt a few got caught and hanged, or flayed alive, or whatever was considered suitable for that offence in those days, but the number of kings' and noblemen's tombs that were not broken open and robbed was zero, and that was all about it. The cash went into circulation again.

So succeeding kings and noblemen took thought. They appealed to the public sense of decency, only to find that there was none. They got the priests to threaten damnation in the next world as the sure penalty for robbing tombs, only to discover that the boys who did the robbing didn't take much stock in the next world, anyhow, but were dead set on getting what small comfort could be had in this. The nobility raised the taxes, strafed whole districts with extra hard labour, issued proclamations, passed laws forbidding anyone below the rank of nobleman to be seen near a cemetery, imported guards from other countries-and all to no effect. Bury a Pharaoh, and the boys got away with his baggage, as often as not in broad daylight, almost before he'd started on his journey to the world beyond.

So they changed part of the plan. It was decided that secrecy would solve the problem. Laws were passed forbidding anyone to know where a Pharaoh was buried. The head undertakers enjoyed a monopoly, and held their tongues for business reasons. Undertakers' helpers came cheap, so they were all killed and shipped along with Pharaoh to be useful to him in the next world. The mausoleum was underground, out of sight, in an unfrequented spot, and the sand was tidily arranged on top to look as if nothing but the desert wind had ever ruffled it. The living nobility breathed again.

But all they had accomplished was to add a sporting zest to what had hitherto been humdrum certainty. The boys had to go prospecting now, and there's no doubt whatever they found the loot, getting away with it all the more profitably because there were no expensive imported guards to be bribed. So the upper classes had to think again.

They did not abandon the secrecy theory. Rather they proceeded to improve on it. A Pharaoh would start to build his tomb as soon as he came to the throne and had finished maligning his predecessor. He constructed false tombs nearby to deceive prospectors. Then, to the real tomb, he had long dummy tunnels driven, leading to a pit, which was dumped full of rock; and on the far side of the pit was the real passage leading to the place where his corpse would lie in state.

But the prospectors soon discovered that trick, and it got so that a Pharaoh couldn't be certain of getting to heaven with a small coin in his jeans.

About that time the easiest way to make money in Egypt was to come along with an intricate plan for an undiscoverable tomb; but as they had no Patent Office, and anyone who had the price could imitate the plans, tombs soon got stereotyped again, and once one real entrance had been discovered it became a comparatively simple matter to repeat the process and open every rich man's tomb on the country-side.

Things had reached the point where Pharaoh and his friends didn't know what the rising generation was coming to, when who should ascend the throne but Khufu, otherwise known as Cheops. He went through the usual process of removing his predecessor's signature from all the public monuments in order to call attention to his own omnipotence, and then proceeded to entertain a distinguished stranger.

Some say that this stranger was Job, the hero of the Old Testament drama. He was certainly an architect and a man of genius. He laughed when Pharaoh told him of the hard work it was for a decent fellow to get to heaven nowadays without arriving like a common tramp.

"Suppose I show you a real idea," he suggested. "If I draft out a plan by which nobody will ever find your real tomb, Khufu, will you give me the contract for the job?"

The plans were produced, and they were marvelous. No doubt there was a cost-plus-basis contract attached with red tape and sealing-wax. Pharaoh signed that, and for thirty years the labourers-the tax-payers that is-of Egypt toiled at the building of what they were told was to be the largest and most magnificent tomb the world had ever seen.

Meanwhile, very secretly and quite a long way off, other workmen were digging the real tomb; and it was into the real one, when Khufu died, that his body and most of his treasure were smuggled, although the public funeral was held at the base of the Great Pyramid, while the population stood around and cursed the tyrant who had forced them to build such a mausoleum for his bones.

The pyramid was so well built, and on such a titanic scale, that the tax-payers, who had built it, knew better than to try to open that; so for thousands of years it stood intact, with Khufu's bones and Khufu's treasure presumably inside. Nobody hunted for his real grave, because everybody knew that he was buried in the pyramid.

But when at last a conquering Moslem, Mahmoun by name, forced his way into the pyramid to get the treasure out, he found it absolutely empty, except for a great stone chest that had no lid. He naturally jumped to the conclusion that tomb robbers had been in there ahead of him. But how I came to know that Mahmoun was wrong and what Joan Angela Leich and the man in the street in the U.S.A. had to do with it shall all be unfolded in the proper order.

CHAPTER II
Moustapha Pasha

I now go forward to the Geiger Trail, one dark night. I was driving a Ford up the winding, seven-mile grade toward Virginia City, wondering at the prodigious guts of the men and women who crossed a continent to tear the inside out of those mountains with pick and shovel. I still maintain that the accident was Joan Angela's fault entirely.

Her Ford, coming down-hill, struck mine very nearly head-on. Her lights were out and her brake-bands burning, so she enjoyed the full advantage of surprise as well as impetus, and it was only a friendly rock at the edge of the road that caught my front axle and saved car and me from falling a couple of hundred feet.

"Why didn't you get out of the way?" laughed a musical voice. "Are you hurt?"

I proved I wasn't by scrambling out.

"Joan Angela Leich," I exclaimed, "or I'm a Dutchman!"

"Why, Jeff Ramsden! Shake hands! I saw you last in Egypt, laying out about a hundred natives with a pick-handle!"

"You got me into that mess!" I laughed. "Here's some more of your doing! D'you expect me to walk all the rest of the way up-hill?"

"You enjoyed the last mess I got you into," she retorted. "Your car's in the way. Push it right over, and I'll buy you a new one."

"Tisn't mine," I said. "I hired it."

"I'll give him this in place of it. This is less than a month old. It's a fair swap. Go on, push yours over."

I made the attempt, but the front axle was bent and had caught on the rock like a yoke. I started to hunt in the dark for something that would do, but she backed her car far enough up the trail to descend again and bunt mine over. I had forgotten to turn off the switch, so the thing caught fire and looked pretty good as it went catapulting down the cliff-side.

"Now what'll we do?" she demanded. "My brakes won't, hold. Think of something, quick!"

I found a place where there was room to turn by manoeuvring carefully, and stood guard at the edge of the precipice while she did the shunting. Then I climbed in.

"Drive up-hill, drop me at Virginia City, and return to where you came from," I suggested.

"Nothing doing! I'm on my way to Reno, and you're the very man I need. Fun going down-hill backwards!"

You need no education to enjoy Joan Angela, so there were compensations. Her granddad crossed the continent in '49 or '50. He was about seven years old at that time, and he crossed the Six-mile Desert on the back of the last remaining mule. He left his son with a claim or two that proved bonanzas; and when the son died he left Joan Angela about a million dollars and a hundred-thousand acre ranch in California.

She had sat on my knee scores of times until either she or I, or both of us, had outgrown that, and then she went traveling. During her absence abroad, her manager, the son of her father's closest friend, found oil on her ranch, so there's no real reason why she should select a Ford to make long journeys in.

She's tall-maybe a mite too tall for some folks' notions-and mid- Victorian mammas would never have approved of her, because she's no more coy, or shy, or artful than the blue sky overhead. She has violet eyes, riotous hair of a shade between brown and gold, a straight, shapely little nose, a mouth that is all laughter, and a way of carrying herself that puts you in mind of all out-doors. I've seen her in evening dress with diamonds on; and much more frequently in riding-breeches and a soft felt hat; but there's always the same effect of natural-born honesty, and laughter, and love of trees and things and people. She's not a woman who wants to ape men, but a woman who can mix with men without being soiled or spoiled. For the rest, she's not married yet, so there's a chance for all of us except me. She turned me down long ago.

"Someone told me you'd gone into business with Meldrum Strange; that's why I was so glad to meet you," she explained as we backed down-hill.

I swallowed that compliment, and answered truthfully.

"D'you suppose he'd sell out to me?" she asked, and again I told truth.

"He feels like a great strong spider in the middle of a web, and he loves the sensation."

"Well, would he let me buy into the firm?"

"Not if he takes my advice, Joan Angela!"

"What have you got it in for me about?"

"We're steady-going, plodding, conservative, cautious, patient, counting on the long swing, and exceedingly careful before we leap into anything."

"Old fogies! Well, would you timid old ladies let me hire your firm for an investigation?"

"It all depends," I said. "We're at the foot of the trail now; you can turn round and go forward."

"Thanks! Depends on what? Where were you going when I ran into you?"

"Can't let mines alone," I answered. "Have to go, look, see. My trade, you know. Had a case not far from here. The man got drowned in Lake Tahoe, and the woman was a poor fish, anyhow; the case against her has just been dropped."

"Who was the woman?"

"A Mrs. Aintree."

"That's funny."

"Nothing very funny about her; she's —"

"It's extremely funny," Joan Angela corrected. "Do you believe in coincidences?"

"Partly. And Mrs. Aintree. So she's —"

"A crook," I said, preferring to put the conversation on a basis of solid fact.

"Um-m-m! That accounts for a whole lot," said Joan Angela.

And for a while after that she sat silent, driving the Ford without lights at much higher speed than the law permits or than the manufacturer intended.

"I'm on the way to Reno more or less on Mrs. Aintree's account," she said, slowing down at last. "She gave a man a letter of introduction to me, and he's in Reno now. Now that I know Mrs. Aintree is a crook, I want this man investigated more than ever."

"What's his name, for instance?"

"Moustapha Pasha."

I whistled. If you go there often enough, and stay long enough, you are likely to meet almost anyone in Reno.

"You know him?"

"Noureddin Moustapha Pasha, of Cairo, Egypt? You bet I know him."

"He's a crook, too, isn't he?"

"I wouldn't lend him a match," I answered. "Is he after your money?"

"No. He wants to pay me money. You remember I went to Egypt. They were having a side-show there, you remember-trying to shoot the King, or to go democratic or ditch the English-sort of five and ten cent revolution. And I hadn't a visa-forgot to get one. I had a hard time getting into the country, and an even harder time to stay there after they found I wouldn't sit still and be ornamental at Shepheard's Hotel. I had to flirt with fat generals, until at last one of them told me that the way to work it was to transfer lots of money to Cairo; then they'd have to let me stay for business reasons. So I did. And I began to wonder what to do with the money. After that I found a statesman with brass arteries who'd do anything on earth if you let him hold your hand and gurgle. He signed all the necessary papers and even invented extra ones. So then I went and bought a lot of land that everybody said was no good because it was too far from the Nile. You remember the piece?"

"You bet I remember it! That was where I had to lay out those fellahin with a pick-handle. Lucky for you I made a side-trip to see what tents were doing in such a wilderness!"

"'Tisn't a wilderness! There's a good well. I never found out why those fellahin wanted to drive me away. I'd paid at least three times what the land was worth, and it wasn't any good to them for crops or anything. However, an officer came along that afternoon, you remember, and conscripted the lot of them for the labour gang. Arrested you, too, didn't he, for being in Egypt without a permit?"

"Yes. It meant nothing in his life that permits weren't being issued in Abyssinia. He took me down to Cairo in a sheep-truck on my own first-class ticket; but go on."

"Well, you know I get notions. I had a notion to see what could be done with that piece of land. About half the Egyptian babies that survive the flies are either blind or going to be. And I knew a number one eye doctor in Colorado, and I supposed if I should build an eye hospital he'd be keen to run it. It was only after I had hired an architect and had the plans all drawn that I learned he had married a chorus girl and financed a musical comedy on Broadway to provide her with a star part. So that was that. And then I had to come home. There's oil on my place, you know, and all the sharks in California, and a whole lot more from the East, were trying to get options on the property from my manager. I wish you'd seen the rush when I showed up! I listened to more black-faced lies and blarney in five days than I'd heard even in Egypt, but they got wise finally, and we've got the thing going in first-class shape now-rigs and pumps all over the place, and our own pipe-line. Never borrowed a nickel."

"Who are 'we'?" I asked her.

"Just me and the manager. I own the whole shooting-match. Well, I kept the title to those acres in Egypt. You couldn't have sold them for a song. I'd about forgotten that I owned the land, although I left a British ex-Tommy in charge of it, just to see that the Gyppies didn't steal the holes out of the ground. However, about a month ago along comes this Moustapha Pasha, and wants to buy the land. I thought it funny he should come all that way, when he could have done as well by mail, but I'd have sold him the property for almost any price he'd cared to offer if his lies hadn't made me suspicious. There wasn't any sense in them. I asked him out of curiosity what he proposed to do with the property, and he said some friends of his intended to make a hotel out of it!

"You could no more make a hotel out of that place than out of a pig-sty in the sage-brush. Nobody would go there. There wouldn't be anything to do if they did go there. It's too far from the railway, too far from the mountains, too far from everybody. When I was using it we had to bring supplies in lorries a whole day's run, and one of the chief reasons why the British didn't come and turn me off it was that their red-tape specialists were too lazy to come and argue.

"Well, I refused to name a price, but told this Moustapha Pasha I'd think it over. He got pretty impudent then-tried to tell me that I didn't know my own business, and that as a foreigner I had no right to own land in Egypt that I couldn't use, and so on. So I gave him the gate. I said if he wanted to negotiate on that basis he could do it through the courts, or through his embassy, or whichever way Gyppies do their long-range cheating. He went off to San Francisco in a huff.

"Within the fortnight, though, he came back I with a letter of introduction from Mrs. Aintree, whom I once knew slightly. Its terms were far more affectionate and intimate than she'd any right to use to a practical stranger, and I grew more suspicious than ever.

"I asked him what he thought the land was worth, and he hesitated for about a minute, and then said a hundred pounds. Wasn't that like a Gyppy, to come all that way and then offer five hundred dollars for a thousand acres? I laughed, so he offered a thousand pounds, and then, when I still laughed, five thousand. He had brought the money with him, too. A draft on New York.

"But there's something about that Gyppy that stirs all the fight in me. His atmosphere suggests a plastered fake. He seems to think he's talking down to you all the time. I know he's a faker of some kind, and —"

"Well?"

"I want to ditch the brute! Need help!"

By that time we were running into Reno. A man stepped out under a street-lamp and held his hand up.

"Driving without lights," he said. "Excuses don't go. Hell! It's Joan Angela! Okay. If anyone stops you farther along, Miss Joan, just tell 'em I said it's all right!"

"You seem popular," I suggested.

"If they knew your dad, and liked him, and know you're on the level, that's all there is to it," she answered. "I'm going to this hotel. You'd better come too."

CHAPTER III
"You talk like the British government"

The hotel was full, but the proprietor surrendered his own suite to Joan, and caused two house-maids, two page-boys, one Chinaman and a darky to sweat furiously. There was nothing whatever to it but friendship-which of course includes respect, or it isn't of the first water by a long way. There were no strings; I saw her bill next morning. And she was charged four dollars fifty for the use of two rooms, supper and breakfast.

After I had found a place to sleep I returned to the hotel for supper. The proprietor came and sat with us while we tackled a scratch feed that his sister threw together in the absence of the cook. For a while the talk was of folk well known to both of them, and of the ups and downs of local celebrities, all worth recording but not bearing on this tale, unless to show that there is a sort of masonry among old-timers and their sons and daughters that is as a sealed book to all outsiders.

You might cheat such people; in fact it might be easy-once. But for all their open-handed kindness you'd never succeed in being one of them until you'd assayed "honest-to-God" before their eyes-after which it wouldn't matter whether you were broke or a billionaire; you'd be on the inside, looking out.

"Anybody staying here named Moustapha Pasha?" Joan Angela asked after a while.

"Yes. M. Pasha. Here a week. Some kind of an Ayrab or something-maybe a nabob-seems to think he owns the place because he can pay. Tips the bell-hops half a dollar and expects 'em to call him 'Excellency' or some such bunk. He's hitched up with a shady gang of lawyers here in town, but I don't know what the game is. I'd layoff him, if you asked me."

"Who are the lawyers?"

"Zezwinski and Zoom."

Joan Angela laughed.

"Zezwinski and Zoom wrote me the other day from their San Francisco office suggesting there's a flaw in the title to part of my ranch."

"Is there?" I asked.

"There might have been once," she answered. "An old friend of my dad's named Collins called my attention to it. It didn't mean anything to him, but after we'd talked it over, he gave me a receipt by which he waived for ever any claim that he might have to any portion of my ranch. It's in my strong-box. Mr. Collins died, and his estate got into the courts. I dare say Zezwinski and Zoom have been hired by some of the heirs to make all the trouble possible, but I didn't even bother to answer their letter. Suppose you ask Moustapha to come and see me in my room as soon as we're through supper? I'll ask Mr. Ramsden to help interview him."

The proprietor agreed, but hesitated: "Is Mr. Ramsden a lawyer?" he asked.

"No, merely white. He'll do."

"All right, Miss Leich, that goes with me. I'll tell M. Pasha you'd like to see him."

"And Tom, don't say anything. I don't want it all over town that —"

"Trust me!"

So, twenty minutes later, the door of Joan Angela's sitting-room was opened by a page-boy, who ushered in Noureddin Moustapha Pasha. The Egyptian's smile vanished almost before the door was closed behind him-the moment, in fact, that he saw me. He had evidently expected a tete-a-tete.

Neither clothes nor nationality appear to me to matter much, and I'm not quite such a born fool as to expect a foreigner's ideas of right and wrong to agree with mine exactly. You can always make allowance for another fellow's standards, provided he has them and believes in them, just as, for instance, a man who makes cloth by the yard can sell it by the metre if he must. But there are men of all creeds and colours, who can mouth morality like machines printing paper money, but who you know at the first glance have only one rule, and that an automatic, self-adjusting, expanding and collapsing one, that adapts itself to every circumstance and always in the user's favour. This man was clearly one of those.

A handsome man, not very dark-skinned, but looking more like a dark man who had bleached indoors than a pale man who had bronzed a little in the open. He was immaculately dressed in one of those grey tweed suits that they get such an awful price for from the men who want to look like wealthy sports. He had a little black moustache, the thin neck of the city-born Egyptian, a rather prominent nose that carne within an ace of being shapely, and bright, dark eyes.

The worst of him to look at was his feet and fingernails; the first were much too small for his height, and encased in shoes that might not have disgraced a woman, and his fingernails were polished until they shone with a feminine pinkiness.

Another way he had of being objectionable was to assume that he understood you perfectly, and that you and he were on a basis of good fellowship merely because he was willing that such should be the case.

"Ah-ha! Miss Leich," he began. "I thought you would come round to my viewpoint; but you needn't have come all this way to see me, really. However —"

"What is your viewpoint?" she asked him blandly.

"That you should sell me that Egyptian property. You have no earthly right to it, you know. Egypt for the Egyptians-that is our motto nowadays."

"And America for any person who cares to come over here and help himself, I suppose?" she retorted.

"You don't suppose I came to this country for nothing, do you?" he asked. The tart note came into his voice as suddenly as if someone had kicked him.

"Nobody ever does," she answered. "If you had come to pay the war debts you'd be a novelty."

She was enjoying the interview, and as that fact gradually dawned on him all the man's acrid jealousy, that is the underlying secret of Egyptian character, began coming to the surface. He threw diplomacy to the winds, and from that moment bore in mind only one circumstance, as his restless eye betrayed-namely, that I was capable of taking him with one hand and dropping him down the elevator shaft. He and I had exchanged no words, but had no misunderstandings.

"I will make my wants known," he said, "and it makes no difference who hears. The fact is my friend Mrs. Aintree employs the same firm of attorneys —"

"Zezwinski and Zoom?"

"Yes. We have compared notes. We were drawing up articles of incorporation of a small company, to be financed partly in the United States, for the exploitation of that real. Estate of which you happen to possess the title."

"Forehanded, weren't you?" remarked Joan Angela.

"Remarkably so. It transpired that legal rights could be purchased which would give the purchaser a claim to that section of your ranch, Miss Leich, on which the most profitable oil-wells have been drilled —'brought in' I believe is the expression. I purchased those rights for cash through Zezwinski and Zoom, who represent the estate of the man who originally owned the rights-an estate now in litigation. My purchase was agreed to by the various litigants, and will be confirmed by the courts of California, I don't doubt. So, you see, I am no longer in the position of one who invites you to sell your Egyptian land to me. I now come to you and say: Unless you hand me the title to those thousand acres in the Fayoum, I will enforce my claim against your California property! You are no longer in a position to please yourself, Miss Leich!"

"Do you think it was sportsmanlike to go behind my back and buy up those rights?" she asked, trying to look serious.

"It was legal," he retorted.

"Do you realize what those rights would be worth, if anything?" she asked him. "D'you mean to tell me you'll trade a million dollars' worth of rights in California against a thousand acres in the Fayoum? Either you know the rights you have bought behind my back are worthless and you're merely trying to blackmail me, or-and I suppose it's possible-you set a higher value on those one thousand Fayoum acres than you do on all my oil! There's nothing doing, Moustapha Pasha! If you think there's any value to those California rights you've bought, instruct your lawyers and bring suit. I'll fight."

He rose from his chair about as lividly angry as a rattler at a picnic.

"I am not a man accustomed to letting my plans be upset by a—"

"By a woman?"

"I shall proceed to enforce my rights."

"Be a man!" she said, nodding.

He was about to make some acrid answer to that when the telephone rang to announce the arrival of a bevy of Joan Angela's women friends, who had only just heard of her appearance on the scene. She invited them all up to the room, so the Egyptian and I had to make ourselves scarce.

"We will meet again," he said stiffly, bowing himself out.

We were only one flight up, but he refused to walk downstairs. He would have considered it infra dig. However, you don't have to agree with a man on all points before holding him awhile in conversation, so I sat down beside him on one of the row of rockers that faced the front window in the lobby.

"Do you know that young woman well?" he asked me.

"I saw a good deal of her several years ago," I answered guardedly.

"Oh. So you are not her friend?"

"You'd have to ask her that."

"Her lover, perhaps?"

"We're all in love with her. It's a sort of religion, or perhaps a cult, in this part of the world."

"What are you? How do you stand toward her?" he asked, eyeing me sharply sideways.

"I'm an acquaintance."

I would have kicked the brute for his insolence, if Joan Angela hadn't notified me that she wished to ditch him herself. One doesn't lightly deprive her of her privileges.

"Do you know her well enough to tell her the plain truth?" he asked.

"I know her a lot too well to lie to her," I answered.

"Tell her this, then, for her own good. In my country I have power as well as wealth; the terms are synonymous in Egypt."

"You need brains over here, if you hope to keep the one or get the other," I answered.

"And it is brains that she will find in opposition to her! I am no fool!" he said, suddenly sitting sharply upright and facing me. "You tell her that! She has to deal with a man who is not accustomed to being refused by women! I tell you, I get my way! I know ropes! When I engage lawyers, they are smart ones, and I make them earn their fees! Do you know Egypt? You have heard of me? Then tell that young woman what you have heard of me! Tell her what happened when an American firm brought suit against me! Perhaps you heard of that too? I could have acquired her Fayoum property without troubling to cross what you call your herring-pond. It is only a question of paying lawyers."

It occurred to me to let him ram his conceited head into trouble in his own way, and then, like the devil in Mr. Kipling's poem, I thought of holy charity.

"Suppose you listen to me for one minute," I suggested. "I won't argue, but I'll warn you. When you're dealing with crooks and cowards, it may be the best plan-although I doubt that gravely-to be a crook and a coward, too. But as far as concerns Miss Leich, you are dealing with another kind of person altogether. Listen to me, now; don't get impatient. I'm going to pin you in that chair and make you listen if you don't act sensibly. Sit still.

"There's nothing to stop you from getting title to that land in the Fayoum except your own indecency. Miss Leich doesn't want it. She doesn't need money. All she would insist on is a square deal. If you happen to know that that land is very valuable-that there's gold on it, for instance, or oil, or something of that sort-all you need do is to lay your cards face-upward on the table."

"You mean she'd sell?"

"I don't know what she'd do. She'd give you a square deal of some kind."

"All right," he urged. "You get me title to that thousand acres and I'll pay you. Suppose we agree on the amount of the commission now?"

"Thanks," I said, "but I'm not in the commission business."

"You want money, don't you?"

"Not at present."

"Well, then, what do you want?" he demanded. "What is your motive in buttonholing me, if you don't want to do business?"

"I'm doing my best," I said, "to resist a temptation to thrash you! I'm taking pity on you if you'd only realize it."

"You talk of thrashing me and of taking pity in the same breath! You talk like the British Government! However, I believe I did not invite you to sit next to me."

Like Dulcy in the drama, I counted ten. It works occasionally. Then:

"It's a matter of common hospitality," I said "You're a stranger in a strange land, and I'm warning you. If you've business to do, you can do it but you'll have to do it straight or you'll suffer; for it simply happens that you've picked on a woman who belongs to a crowd that is honest. And they're so honest that they'll smash you all to pieces if they catch you playing under the table."

"Such hypocrites, I suppose you mean!" he answered, getting out of his chair.

And at that he walked away with a sneer as perfect as a tom-cat's that gives elbow-room, but no more, to an Airedale terrier.

CHAPTER IV
Zoom of the Zee-Bar-Zee

I met Mr. Zoom of Zezwinski and Zoom the next morning on my way to breakfast; he was taking the air with a half-dozen dogs. He believes in keeping himself before the public eye, does Ollie Zoom-enjoys a reputation for giving two-dollar bills to hoboes, provided that someone is looking, and rather poses as the man behind the legislature —a pose that costs him a lot less than running for office. In fact, he cultivates an atmosphere of influence based on clandestine information, and walks to the office in golf stockings to show what a democrat he can be, in spite of everything.

Ollie Zoom likes nothing better than to be accosted by a stranger in the street. It gives him a chance to get off some real, free, genuine Western stuff rather suggestive of a five-cent chromo of the Grand Canyon, or, if you prefer the simile, of a chain-store Camembert cheese, all smell and no flavour. He liked immensely to have me admire his German police-dogs, and told me all about their pedigrees, what they had cost to import, and which prizes he proposed to win with them. They were a melancholy-looking lot of brutes that lacked nothing so much as an honest job of work, but I flattered Zoom unrighteously about them and he grew chesty. When he learned that I was recently from New York he became at once a Colonel Cody in his own imagination. He had asked me pointblank where I came from, which no genuine Westerner would ever do.

"Ah! New York-that's where you see the best dogs, of course, and the best of everything that money can buy. But you can't buy life; that's what I always say, you can't buy life. Out here there's life and lots of it. We're not effete; we're free and easy; there's room to turn around in. What were you thinking of doing out here?"

I answered with one of those true statements of fact that act like bait in a wolf-trap.

"I represent an Eastern capitalist."

The wolf walked straight in.

"Got any connections here?" he asked sharply, suddenly.

"No."

"Well, say-you've come to the right city and met the right man! I'm Zoom of Zezwinski and Zoom-the Zee-bar-Zee, as the boys all call us. Here's my card; suppose you come and see me at my office; at that corner, first flight up where you see that long row of big windows. Light, my boy! That's my medicine. Let there be light! Who d'you represent?"

"The god of good appetites," I answered. "I'm on my way to breakfast."

"Hah! Nothing like this climate for making you hungry, eh? Punish a meal and then see me at nine-thirty! Suit you all right? I'll make a point of being there. There's nothing between the Coast and Utah I can't tell you all about. See you later, then."

He went one way and I the other, but I stopped on the stone bridge that crosses the Truckee River and pretended to watch the water, for the fun of seeing him stand and pretend to fool with his dogs in order to watch me. It was just as well I did that, because Joan Angela came out on the hotel steps and if I had walked straight along he would have seen me talking to her; but he proved less patient of the two, and I remained on the bridge until he turned a corner.

Joan Angela is one of those women who are good to see at eight in the morning. Lots of them look lovely by eleven o'clock, and, of course, in the afternoon and at night they are all adorable. But Joan comes out as if the dew were on her, and is wide awake and full of laughter from the start-hungry in the bargain!

She hurried me in to breakfast with the wife of the man who keeps the hotel cigar-stand, and we three had a table in a corner to ourselves. Joan Angela resumed an argument over the ham and eggs.

"You see, dear," she said, "if you keep on being angry, when your husband comes you'll make him angry too. Sam doesn't stop to think. He'll just use his gun and there'll be trouble. I

23

know Sam's popular and so are you; and of course any jury around here would bring it in an accident, or self-defence, but what's the use?"

"He ought to be shot! He's no better than a coyote!"

"Exactly. Then give him the range," advised Joan Angela. "The law is off coyotes. He'll fall foul of someone whose business it is to go after his kind."

"But think of the brute's impudence!"

She was a pretty little woman, but her eyes were, and her forehead was, all netted up with angry wrinkles.

"Why should you of all people take the part of such a reptile? What is he, anyway? Some kind of prince? Does he think that any woman over here, just because she happens to be running her husband's shop while he's away, will be tickled to death to—"

"Never you mind," laughed Joan Angela. "I've had lots and lots of that kind of proposal! He comes from Egypt, where they think that any woman who shows herself in public is doing it to attract them. They don't know any better."

"He'll learn as soon as Sam gets back!"

"Sam need never know. Why, those Egyptian pashas used to get introductions to me and make me the most amazing offers. It's really funny if you stop to think. There was one of them, a big, fat man like a Turk with a bulbous nose, who swore he'd turn Bolshevist and upset the world if I wouldn't be his fourth wife. I told him he'd better be a Bolshevist than nothing. I called him Mafeesh Pasha-mafeesh means 'nothing' in their language. The nickname stuck, and ruined all his political chance: forever."

"This brute didn't even offer to make me his fourth wife," said Sam's sole partner, beginning to smile at last. "I could have treated that as a joke but—"

"It is a joke. His very name is a joke. Moustapha It suggests a sort of sly tom-cat with stage whiskers. He's not worth getting Sam in trouble over. Would you have Sam get a rep for shooting tom-cats?"

"Speaking of cats," I said, "I was talking with Zoom, of the Zee-bar-Zee, just now. Got a date with him at half-past nine. Are you quite sure about that title to your oil ranch?"

"Absolutely," said Joan Angela, looking straight and frank at me with level brows. She comes of a crowd not given to deceiving either themselves or other people.

So I kept that appointment with Zoom after breakfast, and was ushered into an office hung with pictures of the West intended to convey the impression that Mr. Zoom held options on it all. There pictures of Mr. Zoom standing in the foreground of vast oil-well areas, and of Mr. Zoom inspecting mining properties. And on Mr. Ollie Zoom's great, flat, mahogany desk there were samples of ore that would make your mouth water, if you didn't know how easily such things can be obtained. Mr. Zoom produced cigars and turned his chair so as to have the light behind him, crossing one knee over the other with a sort of "make yourself at home and let's talk intimately" gesture. He had good control of his face; his expression suggested no more than a friendly interest, but the corners of his mouth would have undeceived a widow with insurance money to invest-or so you'd think.

"Now, what are you interested in?" he asked me.

I like to stick to the unvarnished truth; but you don't have to tell all the truth in order to retain your self-respect.

"Just at the moment I have oil in mind, and not in this state, but in California," I answered.

"Couldn't be better! Couldn't be better! My partner Zezwinski runs the San Francisco office. Between you and I and these four walls, a better business head than Zezwinski's simply ain't, that's all. Had you any particular property in mind?"

"Yes,"

"Come on, now; let's have the cards on the table," said Zoom, rubbing his hands together. "We know all the decent prospects in California-every one of them. Name your district, and I'll reel you off what's there!"

"Do you know a place called Arcady?"

"Do I! Eighty-eight miles from Sacramento as the crow flies. Miss Leich's place; that's all of it. No good as a ranch, but they've brought in oil. That girl has millions —'has' was the word I used. Getting and keeping are not always the same thing.'

"Do you know anything about the title to the property?" I asked him.

"Ah! So that's the lay of the land, is it? Well, you're too late, my friend. There's a flaw in her title —a big, wide-open flaw that means she's going to lose a long slice down the middle-about one-eighth of the property, seven-eighths of the oil, or so say men who ought to know. But there's been a man ahead of you, who bought the claim to the title through our San Francisco office. Who d'you represent? If your man has money there still might be something doing. Money talks, you know."

"The man I represent has ample means for anything he sets his mind on," I assured him.

"Um-m-m!" said Zoom. "If you tell me who you represent, so there's a basis of confidence between you and I, so to speak-why, there's no knowing but I might give you the right steer on this proposition. Come on, now-who's your man? My name's Zoom; everybody knows me. I ain't no secret!"

Neither is Meldrum Strange a secret. But if I were to have mentioned the name of Meldrum Strange all hope of worming information out of this man would be gone that instant.

"No," I said; "if you've something you think can sell me, shoot."

He hesitated, but only for a moment. The chance to add more tricks to an already tricky business was too tempting to let pass.

"Well, between ourselves, then. This thing's a wee mite complicated. An Egyptian-he's a prince or a duke or a count or something-calls himself a pasha-yes, that's it, a pasha-has bought those rights from the Collins heirs. He paid a pretty stiff price. We warned him he was buying a lawsuit, but I don't think there's much doubt he can win, and he has already started to form a corporation here in Nevada, to be a sort of holding company for whatever can be won from the Leich estate and some lands in Egypt as well. Miss Leich happens to own both properties, and, between you and I, I rather think he knows what he's doing. I'm on the board of directors of his new company-or shall be when we incorporate, and Ollie Zoom don't lend tame to anything in the nature of an unfilled flush, believe me! Life's too short for taking chances."

"What's the use of telling me all this?" I asked him. "If you've got a good thing you naturally won't part with it."

"On terms, my boy, on terms. I'll always take a profit when I see one. If your man has money enough to buy me out, I'll sell."

"So you yourself have put money into this?"

"Well, hardly; not exactly. My partner and I have put our time and knowledge into it, and that's worth money. We took a share instead of charging him a cash fee. For one thing he balked at the size of our fee, which is a way these foreigners have; they'll pay any price at all for something they can look at, but when it comes to shelling out for service rendered and for legal skill and advice and so on, they yell murder. For another thing, he wants some honest-to-God Americans on the board-folk like Zezwinski and I who have influence behind the scenes at Washington. Now if your man had influence with the State Department this proposition would be his meat. D'you suppose he's fixed so he could make his pull felt in that quarter?"

I nodded.

"You see, the idea is this: this is one of those cases that are best settled out of court, and between you and I, that's what's going to happen. The Leich girl's a fighter from the word 'go'; but I know what I'm talking about. She'll settle, for she's going to get the right advice. Of course, she can lose the best part of her property if she'd rather have the lawsuit; but we're going to offer to take over her whole estate and give her stock and bonds in exchange. In that way she'll be much better off. We'll be more than fair, we'll be generous. The offer we expect to make will cut her actual loss in half if she accepts it once we're in possession of all that oil, with our own private pipe-line to the Coast, you can easily see how a combination with two or three other companies would build us into a concern that Washington would have to take mighty seriously. Get me?"

"But what about the Egyptian end of it?"

"That is the crux of the whole business! The value of that Egyptian property is something fabulous! Of course, it might turn out to be a mare's nest, as anything may in this world, but we'll make enough money from the oil to take care of that, and plenty over! The terms will include the surrender to the company of that real estate in Egypt, and the point is this-that under the laws of Egypt, as I understand it, it's pretty near impossible for an Egyptian to do anything; it's mighty close to being impossible for anyone to do anything unless he's a British subject, with considerable pull at that. But if a strong United States corporation were to take hold of the project with the backing of the U.S. Government behind the scenes, and perhaps a little newspaper publicity to keep the politicians nervous, the British would have to sit back and look on. You get me?"

"More or less. But it doesn't seem to me that you've got that Egyptian property yet," I said: "and you haven't as much as suggested why it should be worth as much as you seem to suppose."

"Well, see here," said Zoom, "I've told you enough to give you an inkling. If you want to know any more, you come across with the name of the man you represent."

"Not yet," I answered. "But I'll tell you this, he's one of the richest capitalists in the U.S.A."

"Do you think from what I've told you that he'll look into it?"

"I'm inclined to think that he will," I answered truthfully, having already made up my mind that Grim, Ramsden and Ross were going to investigate this whole affair to the bottom. "What makes this Egyptian property so valuable?"

"Ah! Now you're asking! Isn't the oil end of the business enough to begin with? If you'll come back this afternoon, I'll show you a map of that property, location of the wells and exact figures. Meanwhile, I'll have a talk with the pasha and we'll have offer ready to send to your man—I take it he's not afraid to talk six figures, is he? And if he likes the look of that, and cares to introduce himself, we'll throw in the Egyptian end by way of bonus-see? We'll go into details about Egypt after he has satisfied himself regarding oil. That suit you?"

Nothing would have suited me better than to learn the secret there and then of that thousand-acre piece of sand, with its one well and its ruinous, deserted, wooden camp. Obviously there was something under those Egyptian acres to send an already wealthy pasha to the States, scheming in partnership with Zoom, whose local reputation was for overshrewdness, that lost him all the honourable business in two states, but had made him a fortune of sorts for all that. Zoom probably knew what he was doing.

So I made an appointment for that afternoon, and hurried back to the hotel to see Joan Angela.

"What do you know of your manager at Arcady?" I asked her.

"All there is to know. Why?"

"Is he in debt, or anything like that?"

"If he needed money he would only have to ask me for it."

"He might not care to ask you."

"Jeff Ramsden, sit down there, come out from behind that mask, and tell me exactly what you mean! If there's anything the matter with Will Tryon, I'm going to know it."

"That man Zoom told me just now that someone is going to advise you to accept a rotten offer for your property," I said. "It must be somebody who's in your confidence. Who else has any say in your affairs?"

"Will Tryon is the only roan who knows my business,"

"How about a woman? I notice you look startled. What woman knows all about your affairs?"

"But that's impossible! Clara Mulready is as honest as the day is long. It's true she knows everything, and I talk ideas over with her and all that. But Clara-why she's true as steel!"

"Are you in the habit of taking her advice?"

"Sometimes. She often gives me good advice."

26

"Has she any money of her own?"

"No. None to speak of."

"How do she and your manager get along?"

"I think Will Tryon hates her. Will is one of those crotchety old-timers who can't believe a woman has more than one possible sphere. He swears I'm the only exception to that whom he ever knew."

"And Clara Mulready lives on the ranch? What is she-Miss or Mrs.?"

"Mrs. She's a widow."

"Any man in the offing?"

"Yes. There's a rather bright young fellow named Jansen. Will Tryon gave him a job on the ranch, and thinks quite a lot of him. He's a year or two younger than Clara, but I think it's only a question of time and enough money before she marries him."

"So Jansen has no money either? Clara listens to Jansen, and would like him to have money. Clara has your ear. Do either of those two people know about the receipt you got from old man Collins that establishes your title to the ranch?"

"Clara does."

"Has she access to your strong-box?"

"No."

"Who else has, besides yourself?"

"Only Will Tryon, and only he when I give him the key and a special letter each time."

"Where is the strong-box?"

"In the bank at Sacramento."

"Has Clara Mulready ever been with you when you went to open the box?"

"Oh, often."

"When was the last occasion?"

"Three or four days before I came away. It's a big box, and much too full; so I took her along to help me straighten out all the papers."

"Did you see the receipt from Collins on that occasion?"

"Certainly I did. Showed it to Clara. There's a little room at the bank for the use of depositors. I little room at the bank for the use of depositors. I decided to hire a second box, so we had both boxes put in that room and divided the papers into them. She packed one box, and I the other."

"Who put away that Collins receipt, you or she?"

"She did."

"She didn't bring it away with her by any chance?"

"No."

"What makes you so sure of that?"

"I saw her stick it in an envelope, and saw her lay another envelope on top of it. She called my attention to it at the time, because the envelope that she laid on top was one that Will Tryon was likely to want before long."

"What was he going to want it for?"

"It's the title deed to a little scrap of land in San Francisco that's as good as sold. We gave a man an option on it. In fact, I had half a mind to bring the deed away with me, so that Will Tryon could take it to the lawyers when he goes to San Francisco. Then I remembered that Will's fussy about carrying valuable papers in his pocket, or even keeping them in the office safe any longer than he must; and he has to go to Sacramento anyhow on the way to Frisco; so I left it in the box."

"Was the envelope sealed?"

"It wasn't. Clara sealed it, and wrote on it in blue pencil what it contained."

"I suppose so that Will Tryon would take it away without troubling to examine the contents?"

"The idea was to save him time. Will's generally in a hurry."

"Now tell me some more about young Jansen. Does Will Tryon trust him much?"

"I think so. He doesn't trust anybody more than he can help. Will is one of those faithful fellows who accept responsibility for everything that goes wrong. Heaven knows how he finds time to do all the things himself that he does do. Now and then he has to trust Jansen."

"Does he ever send Jansen to San Francisco?"

"Oh, yes. That's part of Fritz's business, to run errands. But what are you driving at?"

"The question is-shall we drive or go by train?"

"Where?"

"To your ranch. I propose we give Moustapha Pasha the range for a while, as you suggested at breakfast-time. Are you expected at the ranch?"

"Not for several days."

"Good. I'll telephone to Zoom and call off my appointment for this afternoon. Which is it to be, Joan Angela-train or auto?"

"I've turned that Ford over to the man you hire yours from. Go and buy a decent car for me. I think you're crazy."

So I laid out close to five thousand dollars of Joan Angela's money, and almost within the hour we were scooting along the concrete pike toward Carson at a speed distinctly higher than they recommend for brand-new cars of any make.

CHAPTER V
Zezwinski of the Zee-Bar-Zee

It was characteristic of the woman that, all that long way, Joan Angela never referred to the problem that was taking us in such a hurry back to Arcady. She talked incessantly, telling story on story of the men her father had lived and made his fortune among, but her own affairs seemed entirely out of mind. It was not, I think, that she was counting on me to unravel the problem for her. She has inherited the gift of facing each mile as she reaches it, which I believe was the secret of the conquest of those mountains that we drove among.

If my guess is correct, she had detected instantly the weak link in her line of defenses when I asked her those questions before we came away. She probably saw it more clearly than I did, and faced the situation like a flash. But she has that priceless quality of once having faced it, neither letting up nor worrying until she has met the emergency and conquered it. That is the true spirit of conquest, embodying the said-to-be-unladylike but surely God-made quality described for lack of a plainer term as "guts".

Among such folk as happen to be worth the salt they eat, about the only arrow of outrageous fortune that can really sting is betrayal by one's friends. All else is endurable. Loss means nothing much, provided your real intimates stand by and let you keep your faith in them. Betrayal by mere outsiders hardly comes within the word's real meaning, since the most that an outsider ever did was to take advantage of a momentary lack of watchfulness-annoying, if you like, and mean, of course, but to be expected, and your own fault if you let it happen.

But you've a right-you may say you've a duty to trust the inner guard, as old Confucius knew when he advised the world to look the other way if its neighbour is walking in the melon-patch. And Joan Angela is of the loyal kind whose friends can only lose her friendship in one way. It seemed more than possible that somebody at Arcady had taken that one way, and she might have been excused for nervousness; yet she gave no sign that I could detect of the slightest lack of ease.

We rolled into Arcady long after dark —a dusty, undetermined sort of village, that hardly seemed to know yet whether its destiny was township or collapse. There were ancient trees in haphazard disorder and young eucalyptus set out in rows like armies getting ready for the great advance; old houses built of bone-dry wood, and new ones cut to order out of lumber that still oozed resin; well gear everywhere, whichever way you looked pump-beams rocking endlessly with the intense air of concentration of animals burrowing; and, of course, the smell. They say that's good for you. Maybe. Anything is good for you that keeps your spirits up.

The old ranch-house was a wonder of a place, set far back from the oil-wells, in a fold between two spurs of the hills behind, at the head of the valley, and surrounded by very ancient trees. It had been built in the days when strength meant weight and thickness, and added to by someone who understood that right proportion is the secret of design. There seemed to be absolutely nothing whatever the matter with it, except that it stood so far away from anywhere, and all too close to that stinking outpour from earth's sore wounds.

It more nearly resembled the house that Cecil Rhodes built at Groote Schuur than any other I have seen-a comfortable, unpretending, dignified, and decent mansion with an air of peace all over it-nothing left undone to make it worthy to be lived in and to look at; nothing overdone.

And the first encounter with its occupants was equally reassuring. The Chinese butler must have been a direct descendent of Confucius, for he had all the virtues, including a tolerant smile and an air of not expecting too much from other folk as mortal as himself. Mrs. Clara Mulready was a rather pretty little woman, who looked younger than she was and seemed unqualifiedly pleased-even as pleased as the Chinaman-to see Joan Angela again so unexpectedly. The other servants, who were all Chinese-and there were three of them-did Wan Li's bidding at a sort of automatic trot, like a miniature Gilbert and Sullivan chorus.

Mrs. Clara Mulready looked rather a cuddle-some, caressing sort of little person, with blue eyes and a decided pride of leg that she adorned with expensive stockings. She had a wealth of rather pale hair done up painstakingly, and dimples in both cheeks that danced when she laughed. On the whole, the most remarkable thing about her was that Joan Angela should choose her for an intimate, for the two seemed as the poles apart. Clara Mulready struck me as not exactly stupid but something like a kitten on the hearth rug, too wise to go mousing as long as cream was served her on a plate.

Will Tryon came up to the house to dinner, bringing young Jansen with him. Will Tryon stood up square and grey-eyed, looked a stranger in the face, and cared for neither hell nor hour's as long as the day's work was done and to-morrow's lay mapped out. He had a hard-lined face with a suggestion of the Indian's stoicism at the corners of the mouth and eyes —a rather homely face, but honest to the end of time, and his hollow back and shoulders and loose loins were those of a man, if ever I saw one.

Janson was something different —a rather fair haired Scandinavian sort, very quick indeed with his agreeable remarks, and a trifle ostentatiously respectful-built lightly, rather nervous on his feet, alert, and cut out more for figuring, I should say, or ferreting, than for managing a big concern. You see his sort around legations, doing the detail work and keeping tabs on other folk rather than constructing anything. He wouldn't have made an honest fortune in a million years, I was sure of that, and I wondered what Tryon saw in him; yet Tryon seemed to treat him with considerable friendliness, and Tryon is hardly the man to trust business in a mere human ferret's hands.

They were probably all wondering what might have brought Joan Angela back so unexpectedly, but nobody asked questions. Will Tryon talked with her about the oil developments, and Fritz Jansen flirted half-mischievously with Clara Mulready all through dinner; I wouldn't have given ten cents for her chance of catching him, supposing that were what she really wanted, nor one cent for her judgment if she did. He had his eye on the main chance, that fellow, but I was puzzled about her.

She had one sure virtue that partly explained Joan Angela's affection for her, although only partly, because nothing you can do for Joan makes any difference; she likes you or she doesn't. It was Clara who made music after dinner-Chopin, on the Steinway Grand-while we three sat round the great hearth drinking the divine stuff in. The only fault I find with all out-doors is that its music isn't tameable, as rocks and forests and rivers are; the only good I see in town life is the music you can spread out like a feast of the gods within four walls. It always seems to me that if Judas Iscariot had owned a parlour Grand, and used it, the world would not have slipped backward twenty centuries.

I got no chance to talk with Will Tryon-had in fact no inclination to do anything but listen-until Joan Angela and Clara went off to bed and left us three before the low wood fire. Very shortly after that Fritz Jansen pulled out, making some excuse about early rising, but Tryon stayed on to act the part of host.

We talked about wind in the trees for a while, For the music had drawn that vein uppermost, but I had to broach business somehow, so at last I drove at him bow-on, for he isn't the sort of man who likes suggestions and evasiveness.

"How soon were you thinking of going to 'Frisco?" I asked him, and he looked up suddenly and stared hard.

"When I'm ready. Why?"

"I'll tell you in a minute. Could you go tomorrow?"

"I could, yes. If it was Joan's business I could start to-night,"

"It is her business —

"I'm listening:' he answered quietly.

"Have you in mind to sell a small piece of real estate in the city?"

"Yes. It's sold."

"You have to deliver the title deed?"

"I thought of sending Jansen:"

"Did he ask to go?"

"Yes. He has private business there."

"Joan Angela told me this morning that only you and she ever have access to her strong-box in Sacramento."

"She's most always truthful."

"Then either you or she would go to Sacramento in that case, to get the title deed out of the box?"

"I figured on going. There's other things to see to at the bank."

"You would take the deed out of the box, give it to Jansen, and send him to San Francisco with it?"

"That's right. Joan seems to have been gossiping. She's quiet about business as a rule."

"There's a scheme on foot to rob her, and I suspect the idea is to make you an innocent accomplice."

"Innocent is good."

"To whom is that title deed to be delivered?"

"John Doe. The lawyers who did the business are Zezwinski and Zoom, known all over the West as the Zee-bar-Zee outfit. They're skunks."

"Do you think you could have Zezwinski come here himself and get that deed?"

"I don't know. Maybe. Why?"

"I'd like to catch Zezwinski."

"That would suit me. He skinned Joan once, when she was away in Egypt. What is the idea this time?"

"I don't know, positively. I only know a corporation is already being formed in Nevada as a holding company for this estate and Joan Angela's land in Egypt."

"Say, that's interesting! Who's the hopeful incorporator?"

"A man named Noureddin Moustapha Pasha, an Egyptian of more or less Armenian ancestry. The plan is apparently this: Inside that envelope containing the title deed to the piece of real estate in San Francisco that you have just sold, I think will be found the receipt that the late Mr. Collins gave to Joan Angela. You know the receipt I mean?"

"I sure do. That's what cinches her title to this ranch. Who put it in that envelope?"

"Neither you, nor she, nor I, at any rate.'"

"Um-m-m! I get you."

"The envelope is sealed. I know that. It's all ready, on top of everything in the box, with the contents written in blue pencil on the outside. You might be able to recognize the handwriting."

He nodded. His mouth had set hard long ago, and he was listening to me with his granite-like jaw resting on one fist.

"You get the idea? You would take that envelope from the box and send it by Jansen straight to Zezwinski without opening it. I've been thinking that perhaps it might be better if you were to ask Zezwinski to come here and get the title deed himself."

"He'd smell a rat," said Tryon.

"Can you think of a better idea?"

"Maybe not. I'll take a car at dawn, and get there when the bank opens. Fritz Jansen shall come with me. I'll let him see me take that envelope out of the box and put it in my pocket. Then I'll go in and see the bank manager; and when I come out of there, I'll tell Fritz there's been a 'phone message from the ranch and we're both needed. I'll have him call up Zezwinski, and if it's true that Fritz is mixed up in this, it's a safe bet he'll persuade Zezwinski to come at once before I open that envelope. Then we'll have Zezwinski, and whoever else has had a hand in the business, backed up proper. I hope you're wrong, but if you're right, I'll thank you. Good night. Mr. Ramsden."

I was up with the birds, just in time to catch sight of Will Tryon's car departing in a cloud of dust, with young Jansen in the rear seat. Evidently Tryon was in no mood for conversation with anybody, and he had left it to me to explain the plan of operations to Joan Angela, which

I had no opportunity to do for several hours because Clara Mulready was in her most clinging mood that morning and not to be shaken off by any means.

We spent most of the day riding about the ranch, and I had to watch my opportunity to tell her about Tryon's arrangements. Thereafter she behaved toward Clara Mulready exactly as usual.

Tryon returned about four o'clock, and gave Jansen plenty to do at once to keep him occupied; but I detected one exchange of signals between Fritz and Clara as he passed the porch. She raised her eyebrows, and he nodded; that was all.

Zezwinski arrived in a great yellow battle-wagon of a car about an hour before dinner-time, bragging of the speed he had made, and trying to turn the boasting into flattery.

"A chance to see Miss Leich in her home, you know — a tortoise would have broken records!"

There was somewhere near two hundred pounds of him, all shark. He had a great, indecent nose, too broad at the lower end and much too narrow at the top, brown crocodilian eyes with heavy lids, and a mouth that was all lips-flappy, mobile lips that would have earned his fortune as a maker of grimaces on the stage. It was a big, powerful head on a strong neck, and his shoulders too were powerful, but he was in poor condition, as the size of his stomach testified. His manner, like his partner Zoom's, was that of a man who has adopted the West without being adapted to it, free enough, and easy enough, but deliberately built up from the surface instead of naturally growing outward from a core of manliness.

"Let's get the business over first," Joan Angela suggested, and he was more than agreeable.

"That's right, Miss Leich. Never let business interfere with pleasure; get it out of the way and done with! If you've that title deed, I've got my cheque-book. My clerks will attend to registering the transfer."

We all went into the library-Joan Angela, Will Tryon, Clara. Mulready, Fritz Jansen, Zezwinski, and I. Zezwinski rather wondered at that, and hadn't manners enough not to comment on it.

"Business quite a family affair, isn't it? Well, the more witnesses the better to a straight transaction."

It is an enormous library. There is a fireplace built of Barstow granite, and in front of that, in the middle of the room, a large rectangular table that used to belong to Marie Antoinette, or some such extravagant patron of the fine arts. The evenings weren't in the least chilly in that neck of the valley, but the room was big, the windows were open, and a fire looked cheerful, so the Chinaman had started a blaze. We all sat down-Joan Angela at one end of the table, Zezwinski at the other, facing her; Will Tryon on Joan Angela's right, and Jansen facing him, with his back to the fire. Clara Mulready took one armchair near the fireplace, and I the opposite, for, in theory at any rate, I had nothing to do with the business, and had no excuse for approaching the table. I thought that Clara Mulready's face betrayed signs of nervousness, but Jansen seemed perfectly at ease.

The business didn't take long.

"There's the deed," said Will Tryon, and tossed a long envelope on to the table. Zezwinski produced his fountain-pen and began to write a cheque. I could see the big envelope easily from where I sat. But Clara could not see it, and Jansen's eyes were on the writing of the cheque. Will Tryon's face was an enigma-passive — the face of a man who has drawn three cards to a pair and has raised the bet.

Zezwinski reached for the envelope and tore it open. Then he peered down into it, and pulled out the deed with two fingers, using his thumb, or so it seemed to me, to push another paper back into the envelope.

"Yes," he said, glancing at the deed, "that seems to be in order. You've endorsed it in blank."

He pushed the cheque toward Tryon and slipped the deed into his pocket, then crumpled up the envelope very casually. "No waste-basket? Well, the fire will do."

He stood up to make sure of his aim, and threw the crumpled ball of paper well to the back of the burning sticks, where it caught instantly. I jumped for the poker, and burned my hand trying to grab the envelope before it was consumed entirely. Joan Angela jumped up, but sat down again at a nod from Will Tryon.

"That's all right," said Tryon. "What d'you think you've burned?" he asked, looking straight at Zezwinski.

"Why-my dear man-burned an envelope-you saw me."

"Yes. I was looking to see you do it. Young Jansen here 'phoned you this morning, didn't he?"

"He did."

"He used a desk 'phone in the bank in Sacramento. I was at the switchboard in the back room, listening in. This morning that deed was in another envelope. I changed it. The handwriting on the one you've burned was mine. Inside it, signature upward, there was another piece of paper, wasn't there? You caught sight of the name Collins. That was my handwriting, too. Here's the real receipt that Collins gave to Miss Leich to establish her clear title to this ranch."

Will Tryon drew a sheet of foolscap from his inner pocket and displayed it. It was good poker-Joan Angela's pot. Fritz Jansen's face was ashen —grey, and his fingers below the table opened and closed convulsively. Clara Mulready's face was as white as the dress she was wearing. Joan Angela looked utterly sorry. Will Tryon's look was stern. The only man who showed no particular emotion was Zezwinski.

"Well? What are you going to do about it?" he demanded.

"We'll give you your dinner in the kitchen with the Chinamen," Joan Angela answered. Then she glanced at Clara Mulready, wondering. "Clara dear, will you come with me into the next room?"

Zezwinski got up to go, shrugging his shoulders with a cynicism that I don't think was assumed. He was a shark who had missed his fish, that was all, ready to forget that one and pursue the next.

"Sit down!" commanded Tryon. His voice was like two cracks of a whip, and Zezwinski obeyed.

"Jansen! Get out of here! Get out of California! You've one hour, by my watch, to hit the trail! Take one of our light trucks and a man to drive. You may burn our gas for a hundred miles, and send the car back-any direction you see fit. But don't cross my path or Miss Angela's again! That's all. Beat it!"

Jansen left the room with a sheepish sort of washed-out grin on his face.

Zezwinski rose from his chair again and started to follow him.

"I said sit down!"

Zezwinski glanced at me and then at Tryon, and obeyed. Either of us could have managed him with one hand.

"Now, what's at the bottom of this? Out with the whole story!"

"I've no remarks to make," Zezwinski answered, pursing up his mouth.

"I didn't call for no remarks from you," said Tryon. "What I'm going to have is facts —"

"Facts, eh?"

"You heard me right."

"Well, I'm no poor sport," said Zezwinski, leaning back and thrusting both hands deep into his pockets. "You're talking through your hat, you know. You can't prove anything. I can afford to be generous. What do you want to know? The property belongs to Miss Leich as long as you've that Collins receipt to put in evidence; that's legal advice which I'll charge you nothing. It's free, gratis. What else?"

"Any fool knows why you wanted this place, and why you can't get it," Tryon answered. "What for did you want that Egyptian property?"

"Oh, that's nothing to do with me. That's a side issue."

"No use lying. Ramsden here has had a talk with Zoom. Facts, now! What for did you want that Egyptian property?"

"Didn't Zoom tell you?"

"Zoom's not here. You out with it!"

"I'd nothing to do with that part; don't take much stock in it either; sounds like a mare's nest to me. A client of ours happened to want it. He was so anxious to be in a strong position

33

to bargain with Miss Leich that he paid a stiff figure for the Collins heirs' claim against this ranch. The idea of a holding company for both properties grew out of that. The Egyptian land is said to be valuable, but I've no proof of it."

"In what way valuable?"

"There's some talk about a tomb—a king's tomb, I guess he said. I don't remember the King's name. My opinion is he kids himself."

"There's a nigger in this wood-pile yet," said Tryon. "What I'm going to know from you before you leave this room is: Who corrupted Mrs. Mulready and Fritz Jansen? Who put you up to it, and put them up to it, and linked the lot together? That's what I'm driving at."

"Privilege!" Zezwinski answered. "You can't expect me to divulge a confidence."

"Confidence? You don't know what that is! D'you know what to expect if you don't answer? You won't rob anybody for quite a while if your discretion isn't working good."

Zezwinski didn't care ten cents about divulging confidences. What rattled him was being forced to do it. Being a born bully, he hated his own medicine, and he was no such fool as to doubt that Tryon would make good whatever he threatened.

"If you had asked me civilly, as one man to another—" he began.

"I'll give you sixty seconds!" Tryon interrupted, Pulling out his watch.

"Oh, well-Mrs. Isobel Aintree is the name."

"Her address?" demanded Tryon.

"All right," I said. "I know her address. So does Joan Angela."

"Go and eat with the Chinamen!" commanded Tryon, opening the door and standing back to let Zezwinski through.

CHAPTER VI
"A land in which death is not difficult, but life has its complexities"

High up behind Joan Angela's home, reached by a winding track that in places is barely practicable for a horse, there rises a promontory from which you can get a view of all that countryside. Once on top, you find a level forty acres and about thirty sugar-pines irregularly spaced, great, splendid fellows three feet thick that rise as straight as arrows for fifty or sixty feet before throwing a branch.

On the morning after Zezwinski's defeat we turned the horses loose up there, to nibble and play the goat, and Joan Angela, Will Tryon, and I made a picnic breakfast, which is to other breakfasts as a full moon is to a whale-oil lamp; there's no comparing them.

Below us the whole ranch lay divided into a geometrical pattern by the ugly well-rigs and the dusters of made-to-order bungalows that housed the gangs. It was a strange view, on the whole pretty typical of the birth- throes by which new orders come into being, and I dare say beautiful if you have an eye for interpretation.

Joan Angela was silent. We had seen nothing of Clara Mulready since she followed Joan out of the library the day before, and although, personally, I wouldn't have trusted her in the first place, or have worried about her in the second-and I knew Will Tryon agreed with me-with Joan it was another matter. Neither of us knew what to say to console her, and, man-fashion, I supposed that scorn of someone else might help.

"I'd have thought better of Zezwinski if he'd accepted that offer of a meal among the Chinamen," I said. "He stalked out of the house as if we were the devils and he an angel with his feathers pulled. I'm all in favour of finishing the brute, if we can manage it."

But she could see nothing worth finishing about Zezwinski. "He was never a friend of mine, and I never trusted him," she answered. "It was all my fault. I shouldn't have trusted Clara. I knew she was inclined to be sly in some ways, but I thought that would thaw out of her in time. I guess she was tempted too far. We've got no right to leave temptation in people's way. Left to herself, I think she would have resisted it, but she met that Mrs. Aintree. Mrs. Aintree had been at the ranch quite often when I was away-six or seven times during the past month. And Clara was so fond of the comfort that money brings that she was willing to lend herself to that meanness-think of it! What is the matter with you and me, Will? You always mistrusted Clara; you never said so, but I knew you did, and I resented it. I never thought an awful lot of Fritz, and you didn't like my doubting your judgment. Now you feel as mean about Fritz as I do about Clara. What is the answer?"

"Lord knows!" said Will. "But I know when I'm through with a man, and it don't take him long to discover it either."

That was evidently meant for a dig at Joan, and it drew the first laugh from her that morning. Perhaps that was what he had intended, for he smiled back; but a second later he was frowning again.

"I see she's coming up here," he said discontentedly. "There's no way of giving her the slip —!"

Clara came, looking her prettiest, riding one of Joan's bay Arab ponies, smiling through her tears, but dressed to kill in a glove-fitting grey riding suit. She let the pony go, and came and flung herself beside Joan Angela, face-downward, and then presently looked up with her chin resting on both hands. My guess was that she had thought out that pose in advance, but perhaps I was wrong, for prejudice warps my judgment as surely as sun on the foresight spoils my aim. I started to move away, and so did Will, but Joan shook her head and we both sat down again.

"Are you going to forgive me, Joan?" asked Clara Mulready.

She was plenty good to look at, and if she was acting a part she was doing it perfectly. I didn't envy Joan her job, but Joan wasn't thinking about herself.

"Clara, you don't know what forgiveness means."

"You forgave that robber, Joan-the man who held you up that night when you were driving through the mountains all alone."

"He wasn't my friend in the first place. There was very little forgiveness that he needed. A chance —"

"Give me a chance!"

"Didn't I give you all the chances? I gave you too many, Clara. Do you expect me to forget that-"

"Yes, I do! You can forget anything-anything! Why should you remember my part of it, and care nothing at all about what the others did? You're not even angry with that pig Zezwinski. You don't care about Fritz; you've forgotten him already. Mrs. Aintree doesn't even interest you. Why should you blame me for the whole of it?"

"I don't believe I blame you, Clara. I think perhaps I'm just disappointed. I would do anything, anything, if I could only put you back where you were; but all the king's horses and all the king's men couldn't do that, Clara."

"Oh, Joan, you couldn't cast me off like an old shoe!"

"Of course not. But, you see, Clara, you're no different now to what you were when we first made friends. All along-all the time you've been living here-you've had treason at the back of your mind. That must be, or you wouldn't have listened to Fritz and Mrs. Aintree."

"Well, if that's so, Joan, I've got rid of it! I've cast it out! Joan dear, I've been through hell all night long. I couldn't sleep for crying."

I could have believed that of Joan Angela, but not of her.

"Call me your friend again, and I'll be the truest and loyalest friend that ever lived! You see, Joan, it isn't as if the trick had succeeded; there was no real harm done."

Joan Angela made a gesture between amusement and despair-nothing cynical about it.

"I don't think you can imagine it, Clara, but I would rather have had Zezwinski succeed than learn that you were not my friend."

"Joan, I am your friend! I am! I am! I'll prove it. I'll die for you. I'll do anything."

She broke down utterly and sobbed for several minutes.

"You mustn't cast me off! I won't go! I'll your —"

"Clara, I wouldn't dream of doing that. You may stay here as long as you wish. Only, you mustn't deceive yourself about it. I dare say you have learned a terrible lesson, but so have I."

"You mean, we're just acquaintances? Oh, Joan!"

Joan Angela leaned down and kissed her.

"There. You go back to the house, Clara, and wash away those tears, and play some music, and try to forget it. We three are going to stay here and talk."

Clara Mulready obeyed without another word, not understanding anything, I think, except that she had not been banished away from Easy Street. She did not look back, but caught her pony and rode away down-hill with her head drooping and her handkerchief to her eyes.

"Now, for goodness sake," said Joan Angela, "let's talk of something else before I break down and make an exhibition of myself!"

"Let's talk Egypt," I suggested. "What are you going to do about that thousand-acre lot of yours in the Fayoum?"

"Zezwinski and Zoom wanted it mighty bad," said Tryon. "Mrs. Aintree seems to have her eye on it. So does this Egyptian dude I haven't met. I'd watch my step, if I was you, Joan."

"Mrs. Aintree," I said, "is 'a poor thing but her own'. She has ambition, but can't see straight and keeps out of jail by a string of lucky accidents. If you put a thousand dollars in the middle of an empty lot, she'd tunnel underneath two blocks to get it. Somebody else would get there first, of course, and she'd blame that on human depravity. But she'd be dead sure the thousand dollars was there before she laid her plans to dig, so it's a safe bet there's something in this Egyptian business."

"Why not send one of the boys out to look the place over?" Will Tryon suggested. "There's two or three would like a chance to travel, if they knew their jobs were waiting for them when they came back."

That gave me my opportunity, and I cut loose. "This looks like a case for Grim, Ramsden and Ross," I said. "From what Zoom told me in Reno, I suspect they're planning to commit crime in Egypt and to get away with it on the strength of pull in the United States. That's where Strange comes in. He turns us loose regardless of expense, and as we are known to have no political irons in the fire we get a rather free hand."

"What would you have me do, then?" Joan asked.

"Use your own judgment," I answered. "You wanted to buy our firm the other day from Meldrum Strange! You don't have to buy a car in order to ride in one, though I grant that you did."

"'Tell you what,' said Tryon. "'Ramsden is a man who'll play straight. Why not give him a lease on that Egypt property on a percentage basis? That way you'll keep control, and get what's coming to you, if there really is anything in it. Turn that over in your mind, Joan Angela."

"What I'm turning over in my mind is a trip to Egypt," she answered. "I don't care for making anything out of that property, but I'm curious to know why others should believe it so valuable. Ramsden, if Meldrum Strange will take this thing up I believe I'll lend a hand! Moustapha Pasha ought to be ditched; it's a duty!"

"So ought Mrs. Aintree to be ditched," I answered.

"Oh, hell!" Will Tryon groaned. "I had a hunch this affair was going to lead to a mix-up! Let it alone, Joan Angela! Let it alone, for God's sake! Give Jeff Ramsden a lease, and let it go at that. You stay here, young lady, where the cream's good, and where the worst that happens is a gun shoved against you on a dark night. That's clean danger. Let those damned 'Gyptians alone. That's my advice."

But Joan Angela doesn't like doing things by proxy. Her friendship and her enmities are first-hand affairs, and she is as direct as some other folk are crooked.

"I'll go to Egypt," she said quietly, looking out over the valley as if she could see the Nile in the distance.

"You're looking due west," laughed Tryon, "you don't mean going that way round?"

"Maybe. Might. What's the difference?" she answered. "Jeff Ramsden, do you speak for Meldrum Strange?"

"Within clearly defined limits, yes."

"Will your firm look into this?"

I nodded.

"It's a bet, then! Will, I'm going! I'll meet you in Cairo, Jeff, soon as I can get cleaned up here."

It was the first time she had ever called me by my first name without adding the other. In some way, without her exactly knowing it, and certainly without my deserving it, I had dropped into Clara Mulready's empty place; for Joan Angela is a woman who would wither up and die, like a flower without its petals, if her huge capacity for friendship could not find lodgment somewhere. She seems to me less sentimental than most women; her friendship does not depend on close quarters or constant intercourse, but it's like a rock when she has once placed it. It stays put. She demands nothing of you, except loyalty.

"Give me an option on your Egyptian property," I said. "Give me a twelve months' option for one dollar, and have Tryon write in any terms he cares to. You can have it back whenever you say, but I want it in my pocket for a while."

They both agreed instantly to that, but I laughed that afternoon when Tryon produced the document. It covered four foolscap pages, and protected his young employer's interests in a score of ways that not even the wiliest old claim-swapper would ever have foreseen. I had an option, sure enough, and price one dollar, as agreed; but even if I should exercise it, and afterwards discover a billion dollars on the property, Joan Angela would still have had the control, and ninety per cent of the billion. I liked that man Will Tryon. I have kept on liking him better every time we meet. There's something about real loyalty to an employer that ennobles a man in my judgment, and all the more since there's such a lot of the imitation stuff parading itself for praise.

I caught the train that night at Sacramento, and was in Reno by eleven o'clock. Reno is one of those places where they eat at 6 p.m. and get to bed as soon as the movies are out, but your Egyptian is not so constituted, and, like the leopard, needs a few thousand centuries in which to change his spots; so it was no surprise to find him at that hour sitting in the hotel lobby, very nearly melancholy mad, and being watched suspiciously by a sleepy porter.

He was positively relieved to have somebody to quarrel with, and demanded that I follow him to his room at once.

"You sure ain't goin' to waste good liquor on that heathen?" the porter asked me in a stage aside. "He's one o' these here ar-is-tocrats. Have you heard of a horse's 'hime-end.'"

However, it was the porter's job to run the elevator on demand, and I followed the Egyptian to his room.

"Now," he said, throwing himself into a rocker, "we two can talk business. Eh? You're on the lookout for number one like any other Yank-or should I have said dam-Yank? You seem to know that Leich girl. Perhaps you know her pretty intimately? Eh?"

Don't you enjoy listening to that kind of insolence?

"Go ahead," I told him. "Sure, I know Miss Leich."

"I've been what you dam-Yanks call stung. That brute Zoom is laughing at me. He and his partner Zezwinski played me a fine trick. I paid them fifty thousand dollars for a claim to part of a certain estate, and now Zoom tells me the claim isn't worth ten cents! The swine said it was a client of theirs who sold me the claim, but I don't believe a word of it; they pocketed my money, curse them! And I have nothing to show for it but a receipt that another lawyer told me this afternoon isn't worth the paper it is written on! That's America for you! That's Liberty, Equality, Fraternity-in God we trust —e pluribus unum! That's your screaming eagle, and your home of the brave! Home of shabby robbers and shameless women, that's what this is!"

"Undoubtedly you manage those things much better in Egypt," I answered. "What do you propose to do next? Fight Zezwinski and Zoom?"

"Gr-r-r-yah! Sittin kilab!* I have lost fifty thousand e pluribus unums; they have them, and that is all about it. Ma-alesh! I am not a rag-picker; I snap my fingers!"

*sixty dogs

"What then?"

"I return to my main objective."

He glared at me for a moment with the helpless venom of a beast in a trap. He knew he was helpless, and yet hoped to spit and spite his way out somehow.

"I will either get what I came for, or else make it useless to that Leich woman! I could do that easily! However, I will try the former first. In this land of free robbers there is only one argument that has weight. You listen to the chink of money, and to nothing else-unless it is to the man who makes moonshine whisky, and him you pay as if he were the tax-gatherer! Bah! What a rotten county is this America! What thieves! What hypocrites! Fifty thousand dollars, eh! Well, we will see who laughs last! Now, I will talk dollars to you; that is a language that you will understand!"

"I'll try," I said. "I'm no great linguist. My vocabulary in that language is decidedly limited."

"You know that Leich woman intimately, don't you? Get me the title to that Egyptian land she owns, and I will pay you anything in reason."

"How much, for instance?"

"I am short of cash. Those swine of lawyers have cost me nearly the whole amount of my letter of credit. If it comes to paying her a large sum for the property I shall have to cable for more funds. Allah! You are a Yankee, are you not? Can't you trick her out of it? See here, if you will get me that property for a thousand dollars, or two thousand dollars or so, I will give you a ten per cent interest in it, and you will have made your fortune! Take it from her! She has too much money. I have no compunction whatever in depriving such a wealthy female of something that she does not know how to use!"

"If the land is as valuable as all that, and if I could get it from her, I'd be a fool to part with it to you for ten per cent," I answered. "You're not talking business."

"Am I not? You listen to me! You couldn't use that property. Neither you nor she could use it! Even supposing you could discover the secret of its true value, you would be helpless; for, believe me, I am not a man to be laughed at free of charge! Not in Egypt I am not! Here, these swine of lawyers can take my money and tell me to go to hell; but there, not so! Over there I am a personage—a man of influence, I can assure you."

He looked down at his beautiful silk socks, gathered a sort of courage from them, and continued:

"I am willing to be blind, of course. I understand business. You tell me how much you are supposed to pay that woman, and I will not make too close inquiries. If the sum is not outrageous, I will pay it. Go to her as a friend and offer to buy those thousand acres of desert that she owns in Egypt. Offer her a song for it. Say that you wish to own real estate there in order to bring suit as a resident, instead of as a foreigner. Say anything, but get that property for me!"

"What would you say to an option on it?" I suggested.

"For how long?"

"Twelve months."

"Let me see; twelve months? That might do. An option to purchase at the end of twelve months? Yes, that is a clever idea. Being a woman, she would give an option and deceive herself into thinking that she still controlled the property. Yes, that is better; get an option, and pay her very little for it!"

"I have one in my pocket now," I said. "See here."

And I pulled out the paper and displayed it.

"Mashallah! So you are a true Yankee, aren't you! Is it witnessed? Ah!" He looked down at his beautiful socks again, and polished his nails on his sleeve. "Well. That is worth nothing to you, but a very great deal to me. I will buy it from you. What will you take? I offer you ten per cent."

"You might cheat me," I suggested.

"I? I would not even cheat an enemy! I will deal honourably with you. Listen! Those dirty dogs Zezwinski and Zoom were drawing up papers of Incorporation for a Nevada company to own and work that property. They assured me a Nevada company can own property in Egypt. Now what we can do is to go ahead with that incorporation-employ another firm of lawyers and let Zezwinski and Zoom rot where they sit-and I will give you ten per cent of the shares in it in exchange for that option. Your shares will be worth at least a million dollars in one year's time!"

"At that rate the whole would be worth ten million," I answered. "What kind of idiot do you take me for?"

"You will be an idiot if you refuse to listen to me! You will throw away a million dollars for the sake of the money-hunger that burns in your Yankee breast! One word from me in the right quarter and that whole property is worth nothing to you!"

"You'd have to explain that before I'd attach much weight to the mere assertion," I answered.

He looked at me for about thirty seconds from under lowered eyelids-the long-lashed Egyptian eyelids that have been the wonder of the stranger ever since Abraham's descendants went to Egypt and got stung. They are as attractive as a houri's; deceitful as fame itself.

"In the first place," he said, speaking with his tongue close to his teeth-beautiful white teeth so that the words rasped, "if you were to go to Egypt with that option in your pocket, it would be disputed. There would be litigation and an injunction and the year would expire before you could do anything. In the second place, your life would be decidedly in danger. You know Egypt a little, I believe. You appreciate, then, that it is a land in which death is not difficult to attain. But life has its complexities. Eh? Its risks. You understand me?

"In the third place, failing what is euphemistically termed the act of God, there is the law of Egypt, which is strictly drawn and not to be avoided without skilful and strong influence in high places. In the fourth place-in order that our argument may be four-square, my friend, and you may not delude yourself-as I have already told you, one word from me and the whole value of that property goes up in smoke! I am a man so constituted by heredity, and so convinced of what is due to me, that I would not hesitate to prevent another from getting what I have set my mind on having. I would certainly destroy its value rather than see another enjoy it. So, you see, you are helpless in spite of that paper in your pocket."

It was clear enough that I was not going to extract the secret from him by any amount of arguing along that line, just as it was obvious that the way to learn the secret was to dig-out there on those thousand acres in the Fayoum. There was only one piece of information that really seemed worth trying for in that bedroom, and Moustapha Pasha was such an irritable braggart that the effort seemed worth making.

"There's law in this land, too," I said, "although you possibly don't believe it-yet. I think I know enough about you now to have you arrested and held for trial on a charge of attempted extortion. You might not be convicted by a jury. I don't know. But I'm dead sure I could prevent your leaving this country for a year; and a year would be all I need to look into this Fayoum property."

The keeper passes along inside the guard-rail.

"You would be watched, you know. You wouldn't be able to jump your bail," I added.

"Oh, you Yankees! You all think you're damned smart!" he answered. "Have me arrested! Much good that will do you! I dare say you have not enough imagination to make you dread the retaliation that you will never be able to avoid! But do you, in the fatuous infancy of your foolish, stupid heart, believe that you have me alone to deal with? Idiot! Imbecile! I am a man of importance, it is true, as any ambassador must be. It would cause great inconvenience if you were to immobilize me, as you suggest in your crass ignorance. But-huh-kill me, and you shall see what you shall see! I am one of ten thousand. And every single one of those ten thousand will become your individual, drastic, determined enemy from the moment that you raise one finger to interfere with me in any way!"

Well, I had what I wanted. There was nothing more to be gained by arguing with him. He was only likely to lie if I questioned him further.

"Good night," I said, "I'll think your offer over. See you in the morning, maybe."

If I had been half my size I think he would have tried to murder me before I left the room, but there's a certain advantage in weight and muscle, after all. He knew right then that the issue was joined between him and me to a conclusion-knew it as well as I did.

CHAPTER VII
"The answer is still no" —"Then go to the Devil!"

Noureddin Moustapha Pasha lay abed next morning, and I rode a freight train as far as the edge of Wyoming, where I caught the Overland for Chicago and New York. My next job was to interview the boss and talk him over to my point of view.

It was not exactly easy. Meldrum Strange was in one of his cantankerous moods-feeling the weight of his money and disgruntled at the news of labour wars and politics and one thing and another. You would have thought the French and British had refused to pay their war debts to annoy him personally.

"Joan Angela Leich," he fumed. "She needs husband. She's too wealthy to be at large without restraint. I suppose you've fallen in love with her. Is that it?"

"Yes," I said, "we all fall in love with her. Which class were you in, 1926—or later? Mrs. Aintree is more in the field I canter with. She's somewhere near the bottom of this again."

"The hell! You don't mean it?"

Meldrum Strange is much more easily interested in attack than in defence. Without being exactly a muckraker he is keener on exposing crookedness than on protecting or assisting honesty.

I showed him a typewritten sheet I had found in our record office as we came through. We had been keeping tabs on Mrs. Aintree ever since we took in hand the destruction of her P.O.P. Society, and she was not in a position to do much without our knowing it. She had booked her passage for Alexandria-first-class, special cabin, self and maid-as the last entry on the sheet made clear.

"The sooner she's out of the country the better for everyone, herself included!" was Strange's comment. "We've got our hands full, Ramsden," he went on. "I can't have you cavorting all over the world at the whim of Miss Angela Leich."

He took out one of his black cigars and started chewing it.

"Has she been talking about me? What did she say?"

"She said you're an old fossil. Wants to buy you out."

"Hah! Takes after her father! I fought him for control of the Truckee United. It all but broke us both, but he had the best of it, and he called me a fossil, too. Well, what's in this business?"

Some chance memory of the war between Strange and Joan Angela's father was what tipped the balance in my favour then, for you can't shift Strange from his yes or no, unless some quirk in his own interior turns the trick. Nor can you fathom a man's reasoning. Recollection of that war he waged against Joan's father may have impelled him to keep an eye on her. Perhaps it turned him in her favour; stranger reversals than that have happened. At any rate, he began to listen intently.

"Better wire Grim," he said. "Let him break ground before you get there. You'd better engage your passage. So Joan Angela Leich thinks I'm an old fossil, eh? Tell me, how's she looking?"

There are thirteen lawful ways of reaching Egypt, and one that is unlawful and the best, though not the easiest, unless you know the right men and where to find them in a pinch. At that, you can work it going much more easily than coming; and the secret, of course, consists in making friends, which is less an art than an inclination. I had the luck that afternoon to come on Cappy Rainer at a club that he frequents, and we sorrowed for a while together about prohibition, until he remembered the flask in his hip-pocket.

"It's all right for seamen," he said. "I approve of it for seamen, both at sea and ashore. But for master mariners and grown men in general it's plain hell. That's my last word. So you're bound for Alex, eh? Spending good money on your passage, I don't doubt. Firm's money? Put it in your pocket, and save a week as well. The old Acushla's dirty, mind; we're carrying coal. She'll be out of dry dock day after to-morrow, and the mate takes her round to Philly in ballast. I guess we'll have the hatches on a week from now, and I'll bet you fifty dollars I can name the hour and day we drop anchor in Alex harbour."

41

Well, now you know; but don't blame me if you can't work it too, because, as I said, you have got to know your skipper. They're all great sticklers for the law unless old friendship, which is stronger than all the laws combined, should incline them to have a bet with you.

Grim answered my long cable with two words:

Important. Come.

It was like him to leave everything else unsaid. About all we could do at our end was to watch Moustapha Pasha and Mrs. Aintree, and to wire Joan Angela that the game was on. Strange was against her going to Egypt, on the ground that she would upset the lot of us and make a picnic of what otherwise might be a serious campaign. However, the land in the Fayoum was hers, and she was her own mistress. She wired back to engage her passage by Cunard and Transcontinental to Brindisi.

We kept our preparations quiet, naturally; and we knew almost hour by hour the movements of Mrs. Aintree and Moustapha Pasha. We knew that they met in Chicago, for instance, although our man failed to overhear their conversation, and the day before I left for Philadelphia, who should walk into the office but Moustapha Pasha himself, silk socks, silk shirt, silk handkerchief, silk hat and silky, smooth demeanour! He demanded to see me.

"So you are a detective?" he began, without preliminary. "I have found out all about you. I have a system of my own, you see! I pay someone else to watch you while you spy on me-how deliciously simple!"

"Did you find Mrs. Aintree expensive?" I asked him.

"What do you mean? Who is Mrs. Aintree?"

"I hope she didn't overcharge you."

He nearly exploded, pacing the office floor without a trace left of his suavity, then suddenly stopped and tapped me on the chest with one finger, mastering his rage.

"Yes-since your spies have told you-it was Mrs. Aintree. She described to me how you have hounded her. She told me the nature of your business-the extent of your ruthlessness-the persistence with which you pursue your quarry. Very well. Listen to me. You are business people. I make you a business proposition. I will engage your firm to act on my behalf! I will jettison-is that the word? —my Egyptian partners, and instead of to them I will give my contract to you, fifty per cent of the proceeds from this business! I will let my partners in Egypt go to the devil.

"All you have to do is to exercise that option that you showed me in Reno-keep quiet-protect me from those men in Egypt who will resent my bargaining with you, although I have a perfect moral right to do as I please in the matter-and acquire a bigger sum of money than you ever dreamed of in your wildest imagination! There! That is the kind of man I am! I face issues! What do you say?"

"Where does Mrs. Aintree come in?" I asked him.

"Mrs. Aintree and I intend to be married," he answered pompously.

"Here? In the States?"

"No. In Egypt. I would not marry in this e pluribus unum of a country!"

"What in Heaven's name do you expect to gain by marrying Mrs. Aintree?" I asked him. Knowing her, and appraising him, I was rather bewildered for the moment.

"That is my business and hers," he retorted.

"The question is: Do you accept my offer? What is your answer?"

"The answer is no."

"I will give you sixty-six and two-thirds per cent."

"The answer is still no."

"Then go to the devil! I will fight you! And believe me, sir, I fight with deadly weapons! Good-bye for the present, and later on good riddance!"

CHAPTER VIII
"If you want to bet I'll bet with you"

So it came to pass, as the old-time chroniclers would say whenever they wanted to omit unnecessary detail, that I reached Alexandria ahead of friend and enemy-two weeks ahead of Moustapha Pasha, three weeks ahead of Joan Angela, and exactly one dollar and eighty cents ahead of Cappy Rainer, who likes pinochle. Just as the splash of our anchor announced sunrise Grim stepped off the launch that had come for the pilot, and climbed aboard.

The same old scholarly-looking, quiet-eyed Grim, less conspicuous than ever in a grey civilian suit. The only change that I could detect was a greater suggestion of freedom about his movements since he had left the Army. There were fewer folk who must be satisfied at all costs, and more who might be offended without danger of reprisals.

"Here's a wire that came a week ago," he announced with a grin. "What d'you make of it?"

It was from Strange. Grim had decoded it in pencil between the lines.

Mrs. Aintree and Moustapha Pasha were married in Chicago two days before their boat sailed. Her letter of credit thirty thousand dollars probably exhausts her fortune. She has sold everything she owns except clothes and jewellery.

It was chilly out there on deck, with the dawn wind blowing, and the sky that comfortless pale yellow and grey that Africa makes use of as a mask for her morning mood. We went into the chartroom, and the steward brought in hot coffee.

"Has Moustapha already a wife in Egypt?" I asked. "He's a Moslem, and can legally have four wives here; but that wouldn't go in the States. She obviously married him to make sure of being allowed to land in Egypt. He swore to me that he wouldn't get married in the States on any terms, which makes me think he was married here already and afraid of bigamy."

Grim shook his head.

"He's married. But until she makes a kick, there's not much we can do. He could have been pinched in the States for perjury, bigamy, and Lord knows what else. But I doubt if he could be arrested on a British ship; and once in Egypt he's safe."

"I suggest that we tell her as soon as she comes that she's one of a harem," I said. "She might take the next ship back and save a lot of trouble."

"Don't you believe it!" Grim answered. "As long as she has thirty thousand dollars she'll believe she's clever. She'll make use of him to come ashore, and when the hand's played out she'll simply return to the States and have the marriage annulled."

"Isn't there a law here that can separate them and send her back?"

"If he were a Christian, yes. Not otherwise, until she complains. It's old stuff with a new quirk to it," Grim answered. "There's something underneath that sand in the Fayoum, and I've found a man who thinks he could tell if he chose. The law is quite clear; they can't dig on private property, or remove antiquities without permission. Miss Leich left a British Tommy in charge of her huts, and a jackal couldn't dig without his leave. He has even hired extra guards at his own expense, trusting to Miss Leich to repay him. He's a first-class man."

"What's your clue?" I asked.

"Politics! The Gyppies are all sorting themselves out into parties in preparation for independence, and there's going to be a struggle for power that will make home politics look like a one-ring circus. There's only one thing goes in Egypt, and that's money. The party with the biggest chest will get control. Control, of course, means more money, and there you are. There's a political party that is rather small but very influential. One name's as good as another, and they call themselves the Agrarian Bloc.

"They hold no offices at present, but content themselves with working quietly against any other party that shows signs of strength. Their policy is to discredit everybody and keep quiet about themselves, so that when the time comes they'll be the only outfit with any kind of reputation left to lose. They're nearly all big landholders, and they intend to own all Egypt before they're through."

"Is Mustapha Pasha a big landholder?" I asked.

"He was, but he took a post-war header on the bull end of the cotton market-only just avoided bankruptcy. However, he knows a lot of inconvenient things about a lot of other people, and some of the members of the Agrarian Bloc felt they couldn't afford to have him for an enemy. He's in the secret of Miss Leich's sand-patch. The others raised a fund between them and sent him over to the States with an introduction to Mrs. Aintree and to a firm of lawyers."

"But why on earth to her?"

"Oh, Lord! She's been in correspondence with half the political schemers of the world for years. She's known in India, China, South Africa, South America-it was only a question with her which cat would jump first. I guess she has laid out most of her income on note paper and postage stamps, building up an impression abroad that she's a woman of enormous influence. These Gyppies think she's a marvel."

"Do you suppose she knows the secret of the sand-patch?"

"Remains to be seen. It was probably her idea to incorporate in the U.S.A.," Grim answered. "You see the idea? As the law stands now, whatever treasure might be discovered on Miss Leich's land would be confiscated by Government. But after the British quit, although the same laws may remain in force nominally, it's going to be much easier to side-step them, provided you have influence. The easiest and most obvious way would be to incorporate abroad, and argue that the law can't be enforced for fear of foreign complications. Get me? The loot would line Egyptian pockets, but the Stars and Stripes would be the banner under which the burglars march. That's the general theory of the thing."

"Then they don't intend to dig until after Egypt gets her independence?"

"I guess not. The scheme is to get possession of that land in the Fayoum so as to prevent anybody else from digging."

"But I don't see yet," I said, "where Mrs. Aintree comes in. What do they stand to gain by letting her share in it?"

Grim laughed.

"My guess is the Gyppies intended to use her and then drop her. She propaganded herself to a point where they believed she had influence in the States. They proposed to use her influence, and then leave her to meditate on balked ambition. But I guess she got the goods on Moustapha Pasha, and, by jiminy, her marrying him like that before he could leave the States rather looks as if she were coming to Egypt with a can-opener in her hand! She means business."

"How about murder?" I suggested.

"That's their usual way of turning a page," Grim answered with a laugh. "But she's thought of that. She'll have some way of making it unsafe to murder her. She might easily leave the secret sealed up in an envelope with instructions to someone to open it in case of her death. Supposing they believe she knows the secret, she would only have to let them know that she had done just that. She's much more dangerous than—"

"Let's admit she's deadly dangerous," I interrupted. "What's your plan?"

"Dig!" he answered. "Miss Leich is coming, isn't she? Get her consent and dig. D'you think she'll stand for that, knowing Government will take the stuff?"

"She'll have a perfectly original notion of what to do-and do it!" I answered.

"If they don't get her first!"

"What could they gain by killing her?" I asked. "The property would pass to her heirs, that's all."

"Have you any proof that her heirs wouldn't sell it for a song?" Grim retorted.

"All right. Why not go straight to headquarters? Tell 'em the whole thing?"

"That's what we're going to do," he said, "but we'll have to pick our men. I'll tell you why: it may be a Golconda. The men who are interested are keeping it awfully quiet among themselves, but Narayan Singh and I have overheard some talk, and the figure they name would make the Federal Reserve Board blink-fifty million pounds, or say two billion dollars!"

"Let's hope it's true!" said I.

"Let's hope it isn't true!" Grim answered. "Any such sum of money as that would turn Egypt into Hades! If it's there it means civil war, whoever gets it! With Europe's treasuries in their present state the news of it would drive sane men crazy! We must pick our men and pledge them to secrecy before we tell them anything at all."

"Hasn't the Egyptian Intelligence got any inkling?" I asked.

"Apparently not yet."

"Do you think there's any such sum buried anywhere?" I asked him.

He nodded.

"Why not? Herodotus got his information from men who read off to him the hieroglyphics painted on the outer casing of the Great Pyramid. According to him, no less than sixteen hundred talents of silver, which is the equivalent of about three hundred and fifty thousand pounds, were spent on garlic, radishes and onions alone for the labour-gangs. That gives just an inkling of the total cost. The ruler who spent so many millions-his name was Khufu or Cheops-wasn't spending his last nickel. He had his hands on money, that boy had, and there's no record that he left any of it for the next man. Where did it all go? Khufu suffered from megalomania. Every Egyptian king made plans for being as important in the next world as in this, and they all tried to take money with them when they all tried to take money with them when they the pyramid, and could force gangs of a hundred thousand men to work at it without pay for twenty or thirty years, could conceive the idea of taking a couple of billion dollars with him into paradise. Is that so, or isn't it?"

"You think this money's in the pyramid?"

"Of course I don't. Every inch of space inside the pyramid has been accounted for. There never was anything in there. It's the most monumental bluff in the history, fixed up in every way to look like a treasure-house, or a rich man's tomb. When Al Mahmoun's men broke in and found the passage leading to the upper chambers, the whole passage was full of loose stones that had to be taken out one by one before they could ascend. It was physically impossible for anyone to have ascended before them since the time when the pyramid was finished and closed up. Yet when they got to the so-called King's Chamber it was empty. There never had been anything in it. Khufu was supposed to be buried in it, but he wasn't. He was the richest Pharaoh Egypt ever had. He must have been, or he couldn't have built the pyramid. Where was he really buried, and what did he do with his money?"

"I'll bet you the contractors got all he had," I answered.

"If you want to bet, I'll bet with you," said Grim. "But you're making a fool bet. Do you kid yourself that a man who caused to be painted in huge figures on the outside of the building the amount that he spent on radishes would let anybody beat him out of ten cents? Think again. He was a miser! Do you suppose that a man who could throw that colossal bluff and command all those resources wouldn't be resourceful enough to hide his savings where nobody could find them?"

"Well, who picked up the trail at this time of day, and how?" I asked. "What makes anybody think that Khufu hid his billions on Joan Angela Leich's lot?"

"That's a long story," Grim answered, "and involves flights of higher mathematics that are over my head. It includes astronomical measurements, an understanding of the precession of the Equinox, and Lord knows what else. I suspect there's only one man in the world who really does understand, and he's crazy. I've been trying to get hold of that man for several days past, but they're keeping him incommunicado, and as his name isn't known and he seems to have no friends or relatives, it's impossible to get a writ of habeas corpus. I don't even know where he is. I can only guess."

"How did you learn of his existence, then?"

"Narayan Singh got wind of him. Narayan Singh can go snooping around where I would get killed in a jiffy. Between us we cooked up a scheme to get hold of the old bird, but whether we'll succeed is another matter. He's crazy; that's our one hope. Narayan Singh proposes to go crazy too. He's working up the differential calculus in Arabic. The pyramid is a perfect maze of absolutely scientific measurements that have puzzled the most learned men in the world ever since Napoleon's French commission began their investigation. Nobody could ever dope out why those measurements should be so perfect, and at the same time why there should not be one single mark or figure or inscription anywhere inside the pyramid by way of explanation. They've all come to the same conclusion, however-that the architect of the building, whoever he was, knew more natural science than all the high-brows in the whole world know today.

"It's the only building in the world, for instance, that is oriented exactly north, south, east and west. It bears an accurate relation to the whole earth's weight, and its original height, before the cap-stone was quarried off for masonry for some pasha's palace, was an equally accurate proportion of the earth's mean distance from the sun. There's plenty more; that's only by way of illustration."

"A thousand acres is a whale of a big claim to open up," I said.

"Unless we get hold of our learned lunatic," Grim agreed. "But listen-that lot is in the middle of a perfect wilderness; there's nothing to identify it except the beacons left by surveyors twenty years ago; it's a square of sand with a well near the middle. It stands to reason, then, that if these Gyppies are so sure of its being the real place they're going on something else than figures. They've checked up that old lunatic in some way, and they've seen something with their eyes that corresponds with Something he has told them. I've been out to the property and looked it over. Barring Joan Angela's huts there's nothing but sand and the well. So it must be the well that constitutes their evidence."

"Is it full of water?"

"Up to Nile level. Rises and falls with the Nile."

"How far from the Nile?"

"Thirty miles."

"Too far away for any kind of artificial connection," I said.

"Think so?" Grim answered. "Old Khufu brought some of the stone for that pyramid from hundreds of miles away in blocks of eighty and a hundred tons-stuff that modern engineers wouldn't know how to shift ten miles, let alone set in position. What would forty miles of tunnel mean to a man of his determination? I'll tell you another thing: Herodotus wrote down a story he heard about an underground passage from the pyramid to the Nile, through which the water was supposed to flow into a great tank underneath the pyramid; but the story proved false, for the simple reason that the foundations of the pyramid are considerably higher than Nile high-water. But those old legends have a way of being based on truth."

"Yes," I said. "There was Jeremy's mine in Midian."

"Suppose," Grim went on, "that Khufu was trying to make his real tomb impregnable as well as undiscoverable. To flood it with water would be as good a way as any, wouldn't it? You know that story about the Bank of England having a lake of water underneath it? They did the same stunt in Alexandria with the Catacombs-flooded them to keep out robbers, and to this day the lower levels haven't been explored for that reason; they connected them up with the sea, and you can't pump the Mediterranean dry. All right-the only chance Khufu would have of turning on a limitless supply of water would be to connect up with the Nile. He could start to dig a tunnel forty miles away without attracting much attention, for the pyramid was probably giving the crowd plenty to think about. If he lined the tunnel with stone that wouldn't necessarily cause comment either, because so many million tons of stone were being hauled to the pyramid that, if he diverted some of it, folk might not notice. He could claim he was building a temple somewhere else, for instance. But when the tunnel approached the Nile that would be another matter.

"The banks of the Nile were densely populated; they'd soon get wise to the tunnel, and he'd have to invent a good excuse. Why shouldn't he put a yarn into circulation about a secret waterway from the Nile to the pyramid? I'm willing to bet that's exactly what he did; and I think that when we come to examine that well on Joan Angela's lot more closely we'll find that it taps the conduit that was designed to make old Khufu's real tomb impregnable against thieves."

The conversation was interrupted by a row on deck, and we went out to see Cappy Rainer struggling under the incubus of U.S. navigation laws. They're wonderful laws, but then he is a wonderful man, and perhaps they were designed to give such born Vikings their opportunity. I don't know exactly what had happened, but somebody had refused to do something or other, and had threatened the skipper with the U.S. Consul.

"Go to the Consul, will ye?" he was roaring, standing on one of the forward hatches with his tunic all unbuttoned. "Maybe. But they'll carry ye there feet forward! Get me in trouble, will ye? All right! I've been in trouble scores 0' times. I'm used to it! I'm not one 0' your hot-bath seamen that needs clean sheets twice a week before he can stand a watch. Salt-water's my name, and I'm here to prove it! Hell's whiskers! Why, when I went to sea there wasn't one 0' you bastards would have been allowed to lick the shore-dirt off the third mate's boots, let alone clean 'em. And you stand there and think you'll tell me how to run this ship! Go to the Consul, will ye? Not alive, ye won't! I'll beat your brains out first! Ye think maybe I can't lick the lot of ye? Come on and try, you sniveling dock-rats!"

He peeled off his tunic and threw it on the hatch.

"Come on-any one of ye! Come on, four of ye, then, if one's afraid! I'll take and beat your brains into stuff the hogs won't eat! Trouble with the Consul, eh? Well, you won't live to know about it! Come on. If ye've got guts! Let's see six of ye try and lick me! Let's see six of ye start for shore without my leave, then! Let's see the man that dares refuse an order on this ship! Now then-ye heard me say 'Off-hatches.' Show me the man that hangs back when I count four, and I'll show ye a corpse! One-two..."

It became a mighty busy ship before he started to say three, and then he had to come back on the bridge and repeat the whole argument to Grim and me, with variations explaining what he had said exactly as if the whole harbour had not heard him.

"That's a hand-picked crew down there," he bellowed, as if he suspected us of being at the bottom of the mutiny. "They're treated good, and paid the salaries O' railroad presidents! Clean sheets twice a week-hot baths-hotel Waldorf banquets three times a day-eight hours' work-and three mates to watch they don't do too much! And, barring they're lazy, they're more or less all right until they get near Egypt. But soon as the smell O' this Goddamned country gets under their noses they're no more good than goats in church! I tell ye, Egypt's a lousy cesspool of a country! It 'ud rot the guts of a Nova Scotia bosun! I'll be crazy as a coot now till they see my stern-light swingin' out O' here. You two boys had better beat it.

"No, don't stay to dinner. I'm not fit company for a vivisectionist until I'm out o' this! Go on; pitch your grips into a boat and leave me to stand off the damn fool laws o' the United States and Egypt! I'm a master mariner, I am-nursemaid to a crew of dock-rats and third-assistant- vice-consul's office-boy! Good-bye. See ye sometime, somewhere. Call again when ye want a lift. Push off as soon as ye're in the boat; I'll stand by to kill any o' my soft-sleeping courtesans that tries to jump in after ye! They're as crazy for the shore as sharks after garbage! Good-bye! Good- bye!"

Cappy Rainer was right about Egypt.

CHAPTER IX
"Lent us by Ah Li Wan"

So now you know how you get ashore when you're not on the ship's papers. What explanation the captain makes to the port authorities is between them and the captain. Grim and I, having time to kill until the night train pulled out, visited the tomb called Komesh-Shukafa, whose lower levels are all under salt water. It is a fascinating place, and exasperating, for the splendour of the upper part and the obvious wealth of the family for whom it was first built makes it likely that those lower levels contain treasure worth diving for.

"You see," he said, "when invaders came they simply let the water in. Why shouldn't old Khufu have done that? The care these people took makes you think they had something down there worth protecting. What about Khufu then? These people may have spent a hundred thousand dollars on this mausoleum. He spent more than a hundred million on a mere bluff. Do you begin to see the possibilities?"

I suppose, as a matter of fact, you have really got to be a professional miner to feel the full tug of buried treasure at your heart-strings. Cupidity has not got much to do with it. I don't believe the sight of a hundred million dollars in the open would make any decent fellow forget the laws of right and wrong; but it's another thing altogether to believe that some such sum is hidden in the earth, idle and useless. It isn't gold, but the game of getting out the gold and putting it to work that thrills you and makes you throw dice with fortune. At any rate, that's my experience, and I've been mining all my life.

It exasperated me to have no diving-suit, to go down into those lower levels and explore them made me so discontented that I couldn't carry on a conversation. So you'll understand why I dreamed all that night on the Cairo Express that the pyramid was on my chest, and that old King Khufu was sitting alongside grinning at me just out of reach. I saw in the dream long processions of fellahin, nearly naked, carrying bars of gold done up in papyrus and disappearing with their burdens down a shaft, while the priests of Amen-Ra kept count. And I couldn't get to see where they were putting the treasure because the pyramid held me fast. Then King Khufu turned into Meldrum Strange, and laughed more diabolically than the king had laughed. And after a while the pyramid and old King Khufu and Meldrum Strange and Joan Angela and Moustapha Pasha and Grim and Mrs. Aintree became all mixed up in a mad dance amid a shower of gold, while Narayan Singh and a white bearded, one-eyed lunatic made astronomical calculations with the aid of a planisphere and a surveyor's plane-table. On the whole it was a feverish night, but hardly more so than the weeks that followed.

The very first day in Cairo produced excitement. We drove straight to Grim's quarters, where Narayan Singh had a meal all ready, as well as information that he was almost bursting to impart; but the great Sikh held his peace until after the servant had left the room, and the three of us sat down on the deep corner lounge with our backs against a crimson Bokhara hanging. Then:

"Sahibs, I have found the lunatic!" he began.

He was too pleased with the accomplishment to be self-satisfied about it, but not so swept away by his enthusiasm as not to pause and see the effect on us.

"Thus and so it happened," he went on, when we had suitably expressed our satisfaction. "To look for him was to hunt for one star in the Milky Way. To inquire for him was to be mocked. To set spies hunting for him was to warn the enemy of danger, for the spy is very rare who makes a real secret of his purpose. So, what then? I remembered that he is a lunatic, and the nature of a lunatic is this-that forever he repeats his role. Like the camel that grinds out semsem in a dark vault, he goes round and round, sleeping and waking, one day like another, indifferent to everything except his one obsession. So. And the nature of our lunatic's madness is what? It concerns the pyramid and stars and mathematics. And now another point. As a soldier I have served in many wars. Not only have I fought in nine campaigns, but I have spied; and, whereas any man can fight, or can be taught to fight, the gift of spying is a rather rare one. So it has been my lot more often than befalls most men to venture behind an enemy's lines for information; and according to those officers whose orders I obeyed the most useful information I could ever bring them was concerning details of the enemy's supplies. From that they would deduce all manner of things. So I bethought me, and the fashion of my thoughts was this:

"Wherever that lunatic may be, he needs supplies, of one kind or another. But his wants are surely few in the way of food and clothing, and such as they might be they can be bought at any of a thousand places, and a man might hunt for a hundred years in vain tracing the onions and the roots of garlic from one place to another, and from hand to hand."

"Quite so," said Grim, "now where's the lunatic?"

But a Sikh will not tell his story in any but his own way.

"I knew no more than you, sahib. But I reasoned thus-neither mathematics, nor astronomy, nor pyramids are purchasable in the Fish Market. And a lunatic is often an exacting man. Be he ever so tractable when given freedom to pursue his fantasy, deprived of that opportunity he may grow ravenous, or even die. And considering his importance to the men who hold him prisoner, it occurred to me that they will keep him satisfied if possible. So I turned my back on the bazaars and sought elsewhere, and by and by, on the afternoon of the same day, Jimgrim Sahib, that you left for Alexandria, I found a shop in a quiet street, where a Chinaman sells books on mathematics in many tongues, as well as more sorts of strange instruments than any but he could conceive to exist.

"Old of mutual confidence, he assuring me that Sikhs are brute beasts who make incorruptible but fierce policemen, and I replying that the Chinese are neither for the present nor the future, but are corpses whom the gas of ancient graves has raised into a sort of imitation life. And on that basis we conversed, becoming very friendly.

"And at last, seeing I was patient, he began to tell me how the Chinese invented all instruments centuries before the West had given up cannibalism. And I told him that was like the Chinese, to invent instruments they had no use for, nor could understand. Whereat he began to show me many marvels, and to tell me the use of them, and to lie about what the Chinese had accomplished with such things three thousand centuries before the present era.

"Thus far, sahibs, the trail appeared to lead no-wither. But there was a voice within me that kept urging patience, and you are doubtless familiar with the well-known truth that the only good soldiers are those who are never in a hurry until the scouts have made full report. So, speaking solely with desire to cause him to speak again, I said that the Chinese possibly were living men in those days, but that now they are all dead and incapable of thinking. Whereat, as the way of most men is when so accused, he boasted; and in order to bring his boasting home, he cited instances.

"Said he: 'You see this instrument? Can Sikh eyes see the fineness of it, or has so much liquor dulled the vision?' And he showed me a thing such as I never before set eyes on—a thing of brass that slid inside itself when a screw was turned, so that certain figures came in contact with other figures, and they in turn with more, and there from calculations could be made in logarithms without chance of error.

"Said he: 'You see that, don't you, you whose eyes would rather behold strong drink? You think that was made in the West? Look, see, then-here is the signature of him who made it.' And he showed me Chinese characters cut deeply in the brass. 'This was made in Hong Kong by a Chinaman,' he said, 'and there is but one other like it in the world.'

"Now, as to that, he may or may not have been lying, sahibs; but at any rate I told him he was lying, for, said I, the Chinese forever lie to foreigners. Moreover, I said that the instrument was a simple thing that any fool could design and put to use. Whereat, seeing we enjoyed each other's company, he further controverted me.

"Said he: 'Not only did a Chinaman make that, but none other than a Chinaman can use it. None other understands it.'

"'But the numbers on it,' said I, 'are European.'

"'Surely so,' said he, 'for it was meant that the barbarians should understand it. But none did. For ten years,' he said, 'I have possessed these two machines, and I have offered them at a fair price to all such barbarians as think themselves educated and who entered my unworthy shop. Certain of them were curious, as if they beheld a sort of peep-show, but none understood. It was not until a Chinaman sent to inquire for something of the sort that I found a purchaser for one, so that now I have but this one left. It was no barbarian who bought the other, but a Chinaman.'

"Sahibs, my heart made a leap within me, for the instinct of an old scout assured me I was on the trail. And so it proved. Again I told him he was lying, for any man, said I, could invent a story of a Chinese purchaser and say without proof this or that to clinch an argument. Whereat he took down from the shelf his book in which he keeps a list of purchasers and what they bought and by how much he cheated them and what not.

"'See!' he said. 'Look, see, drunkard!'

"He showed me, sahibs, the name of an Egyptian-Enim Ismail Bey-with an address beneath it that I also memorized, and I inquired since when were the Chinese ever created bey, that being an Egyptian title. So he told me how, not many days since, an Egyptian of that name came to him, making inquiries for a calculating instrument, and how the Egyptian was such a muddle-headed fool that he knew neither the name of the instrument nor its purpose, but supposed that one instrument might be as good as another for any mathematical purpose.

"So, because talk led nowhere, and because the Egyptian admitted that the instrument was needed by a Chinaman who could not walk abroad to make his own purchases, that shopkeeper offered to leave his shop and visit the prospective customer. And to that the Egyptian raised objections, saying he would inquire more particularly as to the nature of the instrument required.

"However, the next day the Egyptian returned and accepted the shopkeeper's offer, and the two drove away to a house in the quarter Tewfikyeh, where was a very old and, so he said, sagacious Chinaman, who soon made known the nature of needs, and the shopkeeper returned and brought the instrument, and made a sale at a good price.

"'So you see,' he said, 'it is only the Chinese who can appreciate such fine calculating instruments.'

"Wereat I said, sahibs, that whether he were Chinaman or not, he must be a lunatic to spend his old age addling what few brains remained to him with any such contrivance. And at that the shopkeeper smiled inscrutably and said that very much wisdom always upsets the human brain, for reasons that no Sikh could possibly appreciate.

"'For as a man grows wise,' said he, 'he differs from the unwise, and in that degree must appear mad to such as lack his understanding.'

"'So your customer was what a sane man would describe as mad?' I asked him.

"'A drunkard would call him mad,' said he.

"'Would a sober and well-educated white man call him mad?' said I.

"'Of a certainty!' said he. 'For the education of barbarians is such that they call all men mad who surpass them in understanding. Yes, they would probably confine him in a madhouse. To you, who are a Sikh and therefore a drunkard without brains, I answer yes, that he is mad; but to a man of true intelligence I would say: "He knows more than any of us"; and in the presence of the sage himself I touch the earth with my forehead.'

"'So he is stark mad?' said I.

"'Stark mad,' said he, 'since we talk the English language in which truth cannot be told.'

"So I knew, sahibs, that I had found the address of the lunatic, and I went off in search of the place and discovered it easily, for it is a big house set in the midst of others in a row, none touching, but all close together-a long street of houses of the better sort, but not so modern, nor yet so well cared for, as in certain other streets near by. The windows are heavily barred, and there are shutters on nearly all of them, and although I watched for several hours, none came and none went through the door that opens on the street.

"So, being weary, and needing time to think, I set certain of our men to watch that door all night. Four men I set on watch, so that if as many as three should fall asleep, there would still be one keeping vigil. And all four swore that none slept, yet that none came or went through that door; nevertheless, that a light had shown until after midnight in an upper window. So, soon after dawn, I myself returned to that street to study the situation fully and conceive a plan.

"There was no light burning then. There was nothing to show that the house was occupied. But it was early, and the tradesmen who deliver milk and such things were delivering from house to house. As I have said, sahibs, those are houses of the well-to-do —of folk who eat luxuriously in the European fashion. Nevertheless, I observed that a man with a basket delivered at the house next door to the one I was watching such things as rice, ghee, garlic and dried fish; moreover that the quantities were small, as if for one individual and he particular about the freshness of his food.

"I followed that man back to the stall in the bazaar whence he had come, and behold yet another Chinaman! But he, observing me to be a Sikh, and having memories no doubt of Sikh policemen in the treaty ports of China, was afraid to tell me anything, beyond that he delivered food at that house daily, now one thing and now another, but always in small portions. I asked him who paid for the stuff, but he answered that one man's money is as good as another's and that it is all one to him who pays, so be that he gets what is due him.

"So I sent some of our own men out again to make inquiries, and within the hour I knew that both those houses are the property of one Zegloush Pasha, a reputedly wealthy man who owns much land in the Fayoum, and that there is a covered way connecting them together from the rear, which cannot be seen from the street because of the shrubbery.

"Now this Zegloush, sahibs, is the same who is said to be the leader of the so-called Agrarian Bloc, whose politics consist in abusing all men and supporting none-the same, in fact, who sent Moustapha Pasha to America. Therefore there is no longer doubt in my mind that the lunatic we seek is secluded in that second house belonging to Zegloush, where they doubtless keep him occupied with calculations, lest he grow restless and perhaps escape and make known his secrets elsewhere.

"In your absence, Jimgrim Sahib, I was puzzled what to do. In this land, as in most others, bribery is the key that opens doors; yet in this case, bribery would likely be expensive, and though I had no fear that you would question my accounts, nevertheless it is not the part of a faithful man to spend his employer's money recklessly. So I took thought again, and went back to the shop of the Chinaman who sells surveying instruments and so forth, whose name is Ah Li Wan-or so says the sign above his door; they lie concerning names, those Chinamen.

"To Ah Li Wan, I said: 'Your miserable countryman, for whom that thing of brass that slides within itself was bought, is in bad hands. Is it good,' I asked,

"So I said to him: 'That old man,' said I, 'remains in that house because he has nowhere else to go; and I take pity on him, having lived in China, and having received on more than one occasion great kindnesses from the Chinese. And it stands to reason,' I said, 'that if he were to be provided with a home more to his liking, among friends instead of enemies-such as you, for instance, could contrive-he would come there willingly. The sage is mad,' I said; 'he loves such instruments and things as you have here, and, being old, he enjoys deference. If you would make a home for him, I think I could contrive that he would come to live with you.'

"However, Ah Li Wan was afraid. He refused to interfere, saying that his business might be ruined if he were to make enemies among Egyptians; but he said he would contribute toward the old man's comfort, if that could be managed secretly. Whereat the gods whom I have always worshipped put a new idea into my head, and I made him a proposal, to which he consented after an hour or two of argument. And the outcome of that is thus, sahib-come with me and behold."

He led the way upstairs, and opened the door of a room as big as the one we had been sitting in-a room that Grim had had no present use for, but had been obliged to rent along with the rest. It was fitted up with almost no furniture, except a truck-bed in one corner, but with such a medley of globes, calculating instruments, and what-not that it looked like a museum almost.

"These," said Narayan Singh, "are lent to us by Ah Li Wan, I signing the receipt for them and guaranteeing the return of all things in good condition on demand. It has cost us nothing;

Ah Li Wan paid transportation charges. So there remains, sahibs, nothing but to bring that ancient here, after which we will flatter his self-esteem and he will tell us all he knows."

"How do you propose to get him here?" Grim asked.

"I have considered that." Narayan Singh looked hard at me. "You, I, and Ramsden Sahib have contrived many a disguise together; moreover, we have risked our necks, and it is not good to let courage die from disuse merely because two of us have left the Army. I will be a lunatic. I will be a Sikh from Singapore, who has gone mad from too much Chinese education. And you, sahibs, will be friends of mine, the one an Arab and the other simply an American, who has traveled much and studied deeply in many lands. Ramsden Sahib must wear horn-rimmed spectacles, and that will be disguise enough. We will call at that house this evening, if you sahibs give consent, and if all goes well at least two of us will get to see that ancient Chinaman. We will have a motor-car waiting in the street, and only Ramsden Sahib will be in any personal danger, and not even he to any serious extent, because he is strong and men will think twice before they offer him violence."

Outside, in the street, a military band went by, playing an air from The Mikado, followed by the tramp of sixteen-year-old boys-for such the British soldiers mostly seem to be in these days. Through the window we could see black-veiled Moslem women elbowing flirtatious, unveiled Levantines, and men of every shade of creed and colour, from Nubian ebony to the thin-blooded white of the fellow who has been too long away from home. A man rode by through the crowd on a milk-white donkey, followed by a string of Coptic monks in single file, stepping aside nervously to avoid motor-cars and offered drinking-water by a man who sold it from a decorated brass jar hung with bells.

Narayan Singh, black-bearded and enormous began to busy himself getting out disguises for himself and Grim. And Grim, in a grey tweed suit, grey-eyed under bushy eyebrows, sat down cross-legged in the corner, leaned against a hanging from Bokhara, and chuckled silently.

CHAPTER X
"Whom Allah hath made mad let none offend"

We spent that whole afternoon rehearsing, not that my part was likely to be difficult, nor that either of the others were likely to misplay, but in order to get the teamwork into it. Grim doesn't have to pretend to be an Arab; he is one as soon as he puts the costume on-thinks, speaks, looks, and acts as if he had been born somewhere east of the Red Sea, with the only difference that he knows more than all the Arabs put together about the white man's view of things. It won't be until a few millions of us on both sides get that gift of Grim's, and learn to see both sides at once, that East and West will ever really meet.

Grim and Narayan Singh between them had enrolled and broken in nearly a dozen good spies, that being mainly a matter of selection in a land where intrigue is the universal custom and spying comes, like breathing, naturally. Two of them kept watch on the house we were to visit, and not long after dark one of them brought word that Zegloush Pasha was within doors. We set off at once then in a hired cab. Narayan Singh sitting with his back to the horses, vulture-fashion, with his bearded chin resting on his knees.

Grim wore a white cloth turban, wrapped around a tarboosh, and all the other dignified paraphernalia of a uleema, or learned Moslem, a costume in which he was sure of getting at least outward respect from anyone who professed the creed of the Prophet. Narayan Singh was also clothed in white-good, well-laundered, expensive linen; for it does not pay to approach the house of an Egyptian Pasha looking like a person who would have to go to the devil if told to do so. The Egyptian aristocracy is one of wealth exclusively, and its manners correspond.

In the more or less dark, at a point midway between two street-lamps half a block away from the house we were to visit, stood the motor-car Narayan Singh had arranged for, with one of our best spies behind the wheel. So we sent the cab away and approached the front door boldly, Grim and I each taking an arm of Narayan Singh and half-dragging him between us, as if he were a cripple as well as daft.

For a minute after we had rung the front door bell we were examined through a pane of glass by a Nubian servant, who finally opened the door about six inches and took my card.

I told him I was a traveller with a problem that I believed would interest His Excellency, but that if he did not care to see me, there were doubtless others who would be glad to know about the matter. That piqued curiosity, and turned the trick. I was invited in.

So I left Grim and Narayan Singh in the hall, Grim on a chair ostentatiously in charge, and Narayan Singh squatted on the floor mumbling to himself and tracing imaginary figures on the carpet with one finger. I was ushered into the library. It was quite a magnificent room, if mere expenditure of money means magnificence. Most of the furniture was from Grand Rapids, but some might have come from the Tottenham Court Road, London, and some from France and Belgium. It was all extravagant, and beastly; but the shelves were liberally lined with books, some of which appeared to have been used a time or two.

Zegloush Pasha rose from a rocking-chair to meet me. He was a rather short, extremely stout man with a politician's smile-little black moustaches, carefully barbered and upturned-little, bright, black eyes set deeply in fat cheeks—a tarboosh at an angle on his close-cropped head-fat fingers-diamond ring on the right hand, emerald on the left-European dinner-clothes, and ladylike patent-leather shoes.

"You have a problem-Mr. —ah-Ramsden? Have a seat, please, and explain. You are American?"

"Yes. But I have a Sikh servant and an Arab friend. They are giving me trouble at present. The Sikh is a man whom much learning has made mad. He's a mathematician, who had his teaching from a Chinaman in Singapore. He and my Arab friend have been wandering about the bazaars together, and have met some Chinamen who said that my servant's old teacher is here in your house. That, of course, means nothing to me, but to my Sikh servant it appears to mean a very great deal. He has been unmanageable ever since, vowing and declaring that he will see his old teacher or die in the attempt. Finally, he threatened to go to the police about it, and actually did start off to do that.

"So my Arab friend and I talked it over, and realizing that we couldn't keep the Sikh quiet we thought it better to put the problem up to you. You see," I said, "he's not sufficiently mad to be locked up, but he's a determined fellow, and he and my Arab friend both swear that they have witnesses who can prove that this old Chinese teacher is in your house. It occurred to me at once how distressing it might be for you if the police were to take the matter up and make inquiries, and it seemed at least possible that you might prefer to let him visit the old Chinaman, as the simplest way out of the difficulty."

There used to be nine wonders in the world. Nowadays, of course, there are nine million; but the most wonderful of all of them is the stupidity of people who let such folk as Zegloush become party leaders. Crowds are not nearly as stupid, really, as the men who control them; yet why do the crowds submit? That little, fat, beady-eyed son of a Turk sat looking at me with every emotion from suspicion to bewilderment crossing his face in turn. He was at a loss what to say or do without a confidant with whom to talk it over first.

"But where did they get their information?" he demanded.

"I don't know," I said. "But they're perfectly sure of it. And, as I told you, my man is mad and not responsible. He talks of accusing you of keeping his old teacher a prisoner; he says he'll get all the Indians in Cairo to come and storm your house. Obviously that kind of thing won't do; no man of influence desires a scandal of that kind. And it I would be so easy to calm him by letting him see his Chinese friend."

"You think so?"

"Oh, yes. All he cares for is mathematics. He wants to talk in terms of calculus again with somebody who understands him. He'll be perfectly quiet if he's allowed to do that."

"This is very inconvenient," said Zegloush Pasha. "Why this unusual hour? Would not another time do as well?"

"As far as I'm concerned," I said. "If I take the Sikh away now, without his having seen his friend, I'm afraid there'll be trouble, that's all."

"Then you yourself do not want to see this Chinaman?"

"Oh, no."

He looked relieved. Egyptians despise Indians as thoroughly, almost, as Indians despise Egyptians. Zegloush would have refused me point-blank; but a Sikh was a different matter.

"Are you a resident of Cairo?" he asked me suddenly.

"No. Here only for a month or two. I'm hoping to send my Sikh back to India, if I can find somebody to look after him on board ship."

"Oh, in that case-one does not like, you know, to have residents of Cairo too inquisitive into one's household; but if this Sikh is out of his wits, and is returning to India, there is really no objection. My servant shall take him to see his friend."

"Better not leave him alone with the servant," I suggested. "Let my Arab friend go, too, and keep an eye on him. I don't want to cause trouble in your house."

"Let me see them both."

I followed him out into the hall, where Grim greeted him with profound solemnity, and for a minute or two he and Grim conversed in Arabic; Grim quoting that Arab text about "whom Allah hath touched and made mad let none offend." In fact, Grim acted his part of learned hajji so well that Zegloush turned and swore at his servant for his bad manners in leaving such a worthy waiting in the hall. And all that while Narayan Singh kept making imaginary figures on the carpet with one finger, mumbling to himself.

"What does he say his friend's name is?" asked Zegloush-not unexpectedly.

That was the one question we had dreaded, but Grim was ready with the only solution of the difficulty that we had been able to think of, and it got by.

"He thinks his friend is in trouble and that he might not want his real name known," he answered. "The uleema saith: 'It is wisdom not to inquire too closely into what does not concern us.'"

"Taib!" said Zegloush; then, turning to the servant: "Show both of them the way."

I followed Zegloush back into the library, and there we sat and talked interminably, he glancing at his watch from time to time with ever increasing restlessness. He was a well-informed and well-read man on the surface, but, in common with most of his kind, preferred his learning done up in nice little parcels to be swallowed whole. He had smatterings of everything by heart, from Aeschylus to Beaudelaire, and could trot out a quotation to cap any argument. But no philosophy, nor any politics, meant a thing to him beyond that Zegloush Pasha must ride the rising wave at all costs.

At last, when we had talked for nearly an hour, he rang for the servant and told him to go and cut short the interview.

"For I have an engagement," he explained, "and I can really not go away and leave strangers in my house."

The servant came back presently in a great state of excitement. Sikh, Arab, and Chinaman, he said, had all vanished; moreover, two Nubians, supposed to be on guard in the passage outside the Chinaman's door, were bound and gagged.

"What does this mean? What have you done?" Zegloush demanded angrily. "Who are you? What —"

He jumped from his chair, shook his fist at me, and rushed by, but paused in the doorway to give orders to the Nubian servant.

"Watch him!" he ordered. "Don't let him move out of here!"

Then he was gone, on the run, through a swinging door at the end of a passage that led into the hall; and the Nubian proceeded to obey orders. I liked that Nubian, for he was a faithful fellow. The disproportion between his size and mine was something not to be ignored, so he stepped to the wall where a shield and scimitar hung between two bookcases and took down the scimitar. But he forgot the shield, so I took that, and it was two full feet from rim to rim, as heavy as so much solid metal. I thrust it out toward him and he slashed at it, breaking about six inches off the scimitar's blade, so then I thrust the shield into his face and strode past, after which I had nothing to do but guard my retreat to the front door-a comparatively simple matter. I was outside in a jiffy, and in the street the next.

The motor-car was gone, but Grim was waiting for me at the corner of the street, chafing his wrist and his face alternately.

"We had quite a job with two Nubians," he explained. "There's a cab, let's take it."

"Did the Chink come willingly?" I asked as we drove toward home.

"He was crazy to come. Talks English. Said they'd kept him in that room so many weeks he'd forgotten how long, and that although they'd bring him almost anything he asked for, they wouldn't let him out for fresh air. Soon as we'd gagged that pair of Nubies we just ran downstairs with him, unbolted the front door and out into the street. I've been waiting half an hour for you."

"What is the prospect of pursuit?" I wondered.

"None. Zegloush won't draw attention to his having kept a prisoner in his house for weeks. But you may bet your bottom dollar they'll do something, and do it quick! They may try using influence to get us jumped on by the Government. They may try murder-poison is likeliest. But my guess is that the first attempt will be corruption..."

"They don't know who we are yet," I answered.

"They'll not take long to find that out. They own more spies, and better ones, than the Government does."

At any rate, we were in for whatever was going to happen, or, as a Moslem would prefer to state it, "that which is written shall come to pass," and the next step obviously was to interview the Chinaman. We found him seated in Grim's corner in the big sitting-room, being waited on by Narayan Singh-a dwarf served by a giant. He was ancient, and astonishingly frail to look at, dressed in black alpaca clothes and a black cloth Chinese cap, with big horn spectacles and thick-soled Chinese felt shoes. Somehow, although a prisoner, he had managed to keep himself shaved and clean, and the fingernails of his left hand were all unbroken, although he had no shields for them. The criss-cross crows-feet at the corners of his eyes, and the cheeklines that paralleled his drooping, dyed moustache made him look good-humoured, and he was certainly not in the least afraid, but smiled on the Sikh's ministrations with the air of an ancient guest accepting what was due to him.

"Since Your Excellency has consented to occupy my most unworthy house," said Grim, "is it permissible to know the honoured name of the great one?"

"Chu Chi Ying," he answered, smiling.

I knew who he was then. Not only Cappy Rainer, but at least a dozen other sailors had told me of the old Chinaman who used to teach mathematics to sea-captains waiting for a cargo and ambitious for their extra-master's ticket. They always spoke of him with wonder as a man who could carry in his head any combination of figures whatever, and who seemed to know such things as tide-tables and the astronomical calendar by heart.

"From Singapore?" I asked, and he nodded again.

"How did Your Excellency come to visit Cairo and to be imprisoned in that house?" Grim asked him.

"Came look-see pylarnid:"

"Wanted to find out who was buried in it, I dare say?"

Chu Chi Ying shook his head violently.

"No man bellied in him. Pylamid is astlonomical monument, and has told one stlory four-thousand year long, but velly learned plofessors all look other way, and teach foolishness. Same as usual," he added, with neither sarcasm nor rancour. "Mathlcmatics saying one thing, plofessors saying something else. I come look-see. I know."

"How did Zegloush get hold of you?" asked Grim.

"He see me one time near pylamid. Must have money. Not much. Must have some. He see me teaching mathlematics to one velly sick man who stop at Meena House Hotel and come sit in sun near pylamid daily. Velly sick man much more sick; go back and lie down in hotel. Zegloush stay by me and talk many questions, not understanding what I say, but his fliend stand by and listen. By and by they talk. By and by Zegloush come back and say, 'You teach my son mathlematics.' So happened."

"You told him what you know about the pyramid?"

He nodded.

"Big fool likee fat flirst mate, wantee master's ticket. By an' by he understand something,"

Well, we fed the old gentleman and did our best to make him feel at home. He scorned Grim's marvellous curry and would take nothing more than rice with a little garlic in it, washed down with copious drafts of tea, but he seemed to enjoy our hospitality immensely and beamed grateful acknowledgment whenever anything was done for him. So, after our own meal was finished, seeing the good humour he was in, Grim pushed a table up against the corner seat, set Chinese drawing materials on it, and we three gathered round to try and get him to expound his secret.

He was perfectly willing. With a few strokes of the brush he drew for us a picture of the Great Pyramid in sections, showing the interior galleries and chambers. He drew it with the swift precision of a man who has studied his subject for years and knows the details all by heart; and then, with the persuasive charm of the philosopher who loves to tcach, he began at the beginning and told us the story of the pyramid and what it meant. Illustrating each step mathematically.

His English improved as he warmed to his task, and he did not seem to mind how often he was asked to repeat a statement or its explanation. But at the end of it-which was long after midnight-although we all three understood what he claimed to have proved, the maze of calculations through which he had led us was still a maze to me and I couldn't have repeated the hundreth part of it. Even Grim-to whom mathematics is, like music, a delight-laughed when I asked him how much he had understood.

"He's over my head. I can't follow his proofs. Yet-aren't you convinced?"

I was, and we all were. As far as I could make it out, Chu Chi Ying's theory was this: There were men in the days when the pyramid was built who knew Knowledge. Abstract knowledge. And abstract knowledge was their notion of the after-life and what we call heaven. Therefore, the attainment of abstract knowledge meant eternal life. But-and here was the rub, as I understood it-abstract knowledge could not be understood unless first concretely expressed in some way. In other words, he who believed he had attained to abstract knowledge had to prove it, and to leave his proof for others to follow if they could. So the pyramid was an effort on the part of old King Khufu to express concretely the sum total of the abstract knowledge that had been taught to him by the sages of his day-who came from abroad, by the way; they were not Egyptians. But that was not all.

Now, mind you, I'm hazy about all this, being one of the concrete fraternity from shoe-sole to occiput. I'm simply trying to set down all that I could gather from the learned lecture of a nice old Chinaman, who was sufficiently abstract to be satisfied with rice and tea, whereas I eat porterhouse steak as often as I can get it.

According to Chu Chi Ying, then, as I understood him, abstract knowledge is infinite, and therefore has no end. One thing leads to another, as it were, and so on for ever and ever. There's no stopping-place; nowhere where you can say: "Here is the end of knowledge, or of this particular branch, of it."

Therefore, he who seeks to express in concrete terms-as in a pyramid, for instance-the abstract knowledge that he has made his own must take care to express its infinity in some way. It must not be complete in itself, but must lead on to something else; and it must in some way provide a connecting link, however obscure and difficult to trace, which other men may follow if they will.

According, then, to that ancient system of metaphysics, however much Khufu might wish to use his pyramid-his concrete expression of abstract knowledge, that is to say-for a blind to prevent thieves from finding his real tomb, nevertheless, if the knowledge he had gained was to be of any use to him in the next world, he was obliged to incorporate in the pyramid some means whereby men might follow him step by step, if they could puzzle It out.

And at that point came in Khufu's limitations, his heathenism, materialism, or whatever you care to call it. He believed, in common with most of the educated folk of that day, that the door of the tomb in which his body was to be interred was the actual door of the next world, and that whatever he should take with him into his tomb, provided he could keep it in there, would be his in the next world also. So unless he chose to turn his back on his beliefs, he was compelled to incorporate in the pyramid some intelligible clue to the whereabouts of his next step forward, which he believed his private burying-place to be.

Does it sound like lunacy? Maybe it was and is. Maybe every speculation on the next world and the means of getting front scats there is lunacy. And undoubtedly our old Chinese friend had got himself accepted as a lunatic by the Egyptians to whom, in the innocence of a craving to instruct, he had confided his discovery. But those Egyptians had been just as much convinced as Grim, Narayan Singh and I were that there were facts and real pots of gold at the foot of Chu Chi Ying's theoretic rainbow.

Moreover, the proof of the pudding is in the eating, and always was. It was possible that Chu Chi Ying was wrong, and that Khufu did not mix his pudding in that way at all. We, who have not spent fifty or sixty years in analysing all the evidence, have a perfect right, of course, to criticize Chu Chi Ying's deductions and to label him a lunatic. But was there any pudding? If what Chu Chi Ying described to us was true, were there any such clues contained in the pyramid as he maintained there ought to be, and if so what were they, and where did they lead?

He laid aside that large sketch of the pyramid that he had made, and drew a map of the Fayoum, showing the Nile, the pyramid, the desert and the distant hills. Then, using the stem of the brushpencil to measure with, he placed with great care a drawing of the Sphinx.

"You know liddle of Sphinx?" he asked, and grinned. "Plenty men know Sphinx made liddle. None guess, beclause not know what liddle is. Liddle of Sphinx, liddle of tomb of Khufu. Samee thing!"

"Then is the tomb of Khufu underneath the Sphinx, or inside it?" I asked him.

"Is point of departure inside ship?" he retorted with a dry little cackle of amusement. "Fat fool first mate wanting ticket askee same question."

He tapped his forehead meaningly with one lean finger.

"Business of think, not guess! You know tligonometly? You know tliangulation? You know what base is? So. Look, see."

He went into a maze of calculations then that would baffle an astronomer who hadn't tables to fall back on. Chu Chi Ying used never a note, set down no figures, hesitated not one second, but reeled off-in English, mind you-numbers running into billions, pointing with the long nail of his left forefinger to the various details of the pyramid's construction as he dealt with them mathematically, one by one. He calculated for an hour. He dragged in the precession of the equinoxes and law of gravity, the speed of light, and the mean distance between the earth and sun, and related all that-in some inscrutable fashion that seemed plausible while he was doing it-to the inside measurements of the empty granite sarcophagus-so called-that was all they ever found in the pyramid when Al Mahmoun's men broke in, A.D. 800. And the long and short of all that was, as he announced triumphantly at the conclusion, that the base of the pyramid on the side opposed to the Sphinx is the base of a theoretical triangle, whose apex falls exactly on the opening into Khufu's real tomb!

"And I go look-see!" he added. "Answer collect. Plerfectly collect! Tomb there!"

Grim asked him to figure out the result on paper, giving the site of the supposed real tomb, but omitting details of the calculations, and he promised to do that the following morning, saying it would take time to draft it out with the aid of instrurnents.

"Have you any idea what is inside the tomb?" I asked him.

"Mummy of dam-fool Khufu!" he answered.

"Anything else, d'you suppose?"

"Heap much plenty money!"

"Any way of guessing how much?"

"No can guess. Can reckon."

"Reckon away then, Your Excellency, unless you want to go to bed."

Now he began unravelling the mysteries of another law that he said was one of the things men understood in those days. It included the law of summation. He said that the arrangement of the stars in the sky was governed by it-of the branches and twigs and leaves on a tree-of the seeds in a flower-of the proportions of dry land and water that go to make the world. He said it governed the proportions of the vases that the Chinese artists made so wonderfully in the reign of the Emperor Ming, and went on to add that it was the secret of all wealth, and of all true architecture, and of all true growth and accumulation.

To him, the pyramid expressed-by means of some abstruse relation between the number of courses of stone and the height and weight of the finished building-not only the number of ingots of gold and silver that Khufu caused to be buried with him in his tomb, but their exact dimensions, purity or fineness, and the order of their arrangement underground. Then, for our special edification, he jotted down on paper the totals in silver and gold in English ounces, and translated that into pounds sterling at approximately current market rates.

I simply refuse to repeat the total. It was staggering. The famous Comstock Lode, with its total output of seven hundred million dollars, was a dwarf beside it, and if there was a word of truth in what Chu Chi Ying undoubtedly believed, then Grim's description of Joan Angela's lot as a Golconda was a ridiculous understatement. You couldn't believe it, for your mind refused to take it in. We three sat back, and two of us whistled; the third, Narayan Singh, grinned foolishly, and Chu Chi Ying sat and nodded at us, much more delighted with his mathematical solution and with our bewilderment than with any thought about the value of the gold.

"No can get," said Chu Chi Ying with an air of finality.

"Why not?"

"Too much heap plenty water:"

"Oh!" laughed Grim. "Let's wake up now and go to bed, or he'll tell us the number of pints of water presently."

CHAPTER XI
"Too much water!"

To Chu Chi Ying mathematics were religion. From the moment the little old man started figuring, and interpreting the figures, he felt himself in touch with the Infinite, and was happy. The rest of us reacted in different ways. Narayan Singh, for instance, regarded the whole thing as a fairy tale, and believed it on that basis; he could gravely question facts that appealed to the Western mind, while jumping at deductions based on argument that most Westerners would instantly reject.

Grim, on the other hand, was noncommittal. Unlike the Sikh, he did not accept the whole argument as proven merely because it bordered on metaphysics; but he did not reject it, even if he could not understand it. Grim was willing to go forward and investigate. I was utterly incredulous after a night's sleep, refusing to concede the possibility of any such mass of bullion in one piece. I knew what a magnet it would be, and how surely men would a magnet it would be, and how surely men would have persisted in their search for it.

"Besides," I said, arguing the point with Grim, "there can't have been all that much gold in those days. If there was, where did they get it from?"

"Why not?" he retorted. "Where does gold go to, anyhow? They had gold to burn in Babylon; where is it? How much gold has been discovered in the world in our day? What has happened to it all? The banks and government treasuries can't account for half of it, to say nothing of what was left by the last generation. Where did all the gold go that Spain won from Mexico and South America? If the stuff can disappear out of circulation nowadays, it certainly could then, with an autocrat like Khufu doing what he darn well pleased. If he could tell off a hundred thousand men to build a pyramid, he could send another hundred thousand to the mines, for that matter; and the world is chock-a-block with ancient workings that nobody can set a date to or explain. If there's any gold at all in Khufu's tomb there may just as easily be a whale of a lot. Let's go look."

There was nothing much that we could actually do, of course, until Joan Angela's arrival. On the other hand, there was nothing to be gained by hanging around in Cairo, where we might prove easy marks for Zegloush and his gang. So we hired a big car, and persuaded Chu Chi Ying to come with us. We started an hour after dawn, and none of us noticed any spies lurking near the house; but what we did see, as we sped toward the outskirts of the city, were extremely obvious signs of discontent — mobs gathering even at that hour, and furious spellbinders haranguing them from windows.

Our Western mob-orators are mere dead-heads compared to the agitators of the East, and for producing quick action they are as oxen compared to petrol. We began to be pelted with rocks. The windscreen was smashed before we were out of the city. We heard the bugles blowing at the Citadel to announce that Tommy Atkins was turning out to his ancient duty of restoring order.

I don't think even Grim quite realized, as yet, the extent of the influence of that Agrarian Blocc that Zegloush nominally controlled. The mob was turned. Out for no other purpose than to provide a screen behind which to invade our quarters, although the story they told to arouse the mob was that the British had purposely reduced the price of cotton in order to impoverish Egypt and keep the country that much more easily in subjection. Our quarters was the only place raided and searched.

In blissful ignorance of all that, we bowled out along the good macadam pike under the overarching lebbakh-trees as far as the Great Pyramid, and then struck out across the desert with the Sphinx behind us. Chu Chi Ying had not had time to draw his map for us, but there was no doubt of the direction, for there were still traces here and there of the track made by Joan Angela's lorries. Several tracks, in fact, converged toward that land of hers, for the well was the only one for scores of miles at which sweet water could be had without payment.

We had to drive slowly for fear of shaking Chu Chi Ying to pieces, so it was nearly noon when we reached the sun-dried, unpainted buildings and were accosted by a man in a blue shirt with blue powdermarks all over his face, and an unmistakable air of delegated authority. His back was truculent, and his Cockney face suggested the uncompromising impudence of drawn brass. He gave us a taste of his temper before he recognized Grim, for his eyes were the worse for blinking across sun-baked desert.

"You can 'ave water for yer raiatord, and then sling yer bloomin' 'ooks. The howner o' this plaice don't allow no trespassin', so now yer know. The 'uts ain't for sale, nor yet the land neither. My orders are to warn everybody off. Can yer read that notice? Ow! It's you, sir, is it? News 0' Miss Leich, by any chance?"

He was a strange cuss. He had six Gyppies there, whom he had paid out of his own pocket hitherto, to help him guard the place, and he had drilled them so that they jumped to attention whenever he moved his head. There was not a nail missing; he had kept the blown sand shovelled clear; and although paint was lacking, and much of the woodwork had cracked in the dry heat, the camp was as ready for use as faithful obstinacy had been able to contrive. Even the cheap brass door-knobs were clean and bright, and the only liberty he had taken with his employer's property had been to break up some benches to construct a water-trough beside the well. He apologized for it.

"There weren't no other wye, sir, 0' gettin' these 'ere Harabs an' their camels watered and off the lot.' They was near drivin' me crazy, 'angin' round all day dippin' out water a quart at a time."

That provided us with a perfect excuse for examining the well without taking him into our confidence. The well stood practically in the centre of the camp with buildings on three sides of it, and beside the old-fashioned bucket and beam arrangement, there was a motor pump installed by Joan Angela's direction; but the pump had long been out of order, and Grim suggested putting it to rights.

The well had a score of remarkable features. It was not especially deep; a plumb-line touched bottom at thirty-five feet below water-level, and the water at that time was fifteen feet below the surface. The maximum diameter was slightly more than six feet, and there seemed to be no cistern at the bottom; nevertheless, the supply of water was apparently inexhaustible, for, however much was pumped out, it was said never to make any difference to the level, which responded only to the rise and fall of the Nile, forty miles away.

Then there were the stones of which the shaft was made. Those at the top were obviously old stones that had been found in disorder and replaced with cement fairly recently; most of them had been broken and suggested nothing more than makeshift masonry. But commencing about eight below the ground-level the courses were great, carefully squared blocks, so marvellously laid in place that, from above, the looked almost like a (...) with one foot in the bucket, under pretext of examining the iron suction-pipe belonging to the motor pump, and it was only with the utmost difficulty that I could trace the joints between the courses. Even at the corners I could not find a crack with the aid of a knife-blade.

Chu Chi Ying appeared to think we were bent on exploration there and then, and borrowing my fountain-pen he drew a diagram of the well-shaft, showing that what we supposed to be the bottom should really be no more than a sharp turn, beyond which, according to his theory, the shaft continued downward at an angle of twenty-five degrees.

"Same angle inside pylamid," he explained.

"Twenty-six minutes, four seconds." I determined on a long chance, and hunted for a big rock to put in the well-bucket. Having found that, I stripped my clothes off, once again set one foot on the bucket, and, clinging to the rope, told the others to let go suddenly when I gave the signal, and not to 'haul up again until I jerked the rope violently.

With my head just out of water, waiting to give the signal, I began to have an absurd dread of crocodiles! There was not one chance in a thousand billion but the suggestion became so strong that if I had waited another minute I would have funked it!

At any rate, I took a long breath, raised my left hand, and plunged under, holding my nose in my left hand, after the sponge-diver fashion, and that fact contributed to the genuine danger as soon as I touched bottom. For, as Chu Chi Ying had predicted, the bottom was not flat, but at an angle, and the bucket did not hit the stonework square, but edgewise, my feet thrusting it forward as I clung with one hand to the rope; so that in a second I was shooting away down into the dark again on a slippery, stone, underwater ramp, striking out with my left hand too late to catch the edge overhead.

I did not dare let go of rope or bucket, for the stone was so slippery that to scramble back up the ramp would have been impossible. On the other hand, I could not signal, as agreed on, without letting go; so there was nothing else for it but to slide on down into black darkness, hoping that Grim would take alarm and haul short before the end of the rope should slip over the beam, or my breath give out. At a pinch my supply of breath was good for about two minutes, but it seemed like two hours before the rope tightened with a jerk and I felt the strain as they started to try to haul me up again.

They hauled so hard that the half-inch manila rope looked like breaking. Nothing happened! I could see nothing-not even light up above me; but I could feel that the bucket was caught on the edge of a sharp stone corner where the ramp left off and the masonry fell away vertically. I kicked and struggled, but failed to shift it. The harder I kicked, the tighter it stuck, and every effort only lessened my remaining breath. I did not dare strain on the rope too hard, for my weight added to their pull might cut it asunder overhead, where it chafed against the stone corner. In desperation I took a longer chance than ever, and forced my way downward until I could get the bucket in both hands and shake it loose.

By that time I was in no fit state to do what Narayan Singh would have termed scouting. The bucket came away suddenly and carried me upward, feet-first, until my feet struck the sharp corner overhead and I had no more strength left for fending my body away from the stonework. I don't know what happened then, exactly, only that I clung to the bucket so desperately that when I reached the surface, half-unconscious, they could hardly pry my fingers loose from it. For about ten minutes I could not remember what had taken place below water, and was aware of nothing but the pain caused by being bruised and scraped against the rock. But Joan Angela's Tommy Atkins-his name was really Atkins-had some oil that eased the pain considerably, and after a while I was able to describe what had happened.

"Chu Chi Ying is right," Grim commented.

"Mathlematics light, not Chu Chi Ying," the old fellow answered. "Look, see."

He set to work and drew another diagram, purporting to show the whole arrangement of the abyss that I had nearly been drowned in. According to his drawing, Khufu's tomb was a good-sized island, surrounded and covered by water, and with a cavern underneath it, full of water too, so that anyone attempting to burrow up from below would be swamped as soon as he pierced the masonry floor.

"Too much water!" he said pleasantly, as if the knowledge gave him private satisfaction.

"Which way does the water flow in?" Grim demanded, and, without a second's hesitation, Chu Chi Ying connected up the Nile and the well on paper with one sweep of the pen. I have reproduced his drawing as I recall it. Grim kept the original.

By that time it was no use trying to keep the secret from Atkins.

"Struth!" he remarked, looking at the drawing over Grim's shoulder. "Hi thought as 'ow there was some uncommon partic'lar reason why these Gyppies was so set on gettin' rid 0' me. So that's the gime! A bloomin' sepulchre! Say-see the blighter's cunnin' little stratagem? 'E set that well where it is, so's anybody 'ud waste ten years 'untin' for a tunnel leadin' from the well to the bloomin' Nile! Well, I'll be damned if 'e 'asn't let the water in the other end an' taken 'is tunnel a mile round in a circuit. D'yer s'pose that old Chink's crazy, or does 'e know what 'e's crackin' on about?"

Grim drew a copy of Chu Chi Ying's plan, and gave the copy to Atkins.

"Don't show that to anyone," he said. "Eat it before you let anyone get hold of it. Spend your time trying to trace that water-tunnel. If we' can find that we can dig down and cut it; and once we've plugged it, pumping out the water will be simply a question of time. Prospect around a bit, and put your six men on to digging, but pitch a marquee over the spot, and carefully spread the sand you take out. If you need lumber to shore up the hole with, pull down partitions from inside the huts. I'll give you that in writing so's to make you all square with Miss Leich."

We drove away, leaving Atkins well contented. To be trusted was the height of his ambition, and he shrewdly realized that his employer would reward him far more liberally for keeping the secret than any Egyptian would bribe him for betraying it.

We were much less contented than Atkins was by the time we drew abreast of Gizeh, for a rifleshot cracked out from among the sand-dunes and the bullet went through the top of Chu Chi Ying's black cap, which was close enough. Evidently orders had been given to prevent our making use of the little old Chinaman on the "dead men tell no secrets" principle.

He was such a talkative, kindly little fellow, that, although he professed not to be sure how much he had told to Zegloush, it was a fairly safe bet that he had told everything. Zegloush, or someone in his confidence, had almost certainly made notes, so that the Egyptians probably stood to lose less than nothing by the Chinaman's death, whereas he might not yet have had time to tell us all he knew.

Two servants, aided by our corps of spies, had restored our quarters to fair order before we got home, and nothing appeared to have been stolen. As a rule a mob tears down everything within reach. According to our servants' account, there had been a great disturbance in the street below, with crowds breaking open cupboards, but finding nothing that contented them. They said nothing-did nothing, except hunt high and low, and it probably would have fared ill with Chu Chi Ying if they had I caught him under our roof.

So Grim got busy and worked out a plan of defence, which included the cook's tasting in our presence every dish of food that he set before us. The fat, black rascal was prodigiously amused by that precaution; he was probably faithful, but certainly lazy like all the rest of them, and the knowledge that he had to take that risk three times a day did more to keep him on the qui vive than any amount of talking could have accomplished.

We might have called in the police, but that would have involved explanations that we did not care to make as yet. We decided to keep silence until after Joan Angela's arrival, and let her make whatever disposition she might please of her own property. The Government would have to be informed before anything practical could be done toward opening Khufu's tomb, but it was clearly her right to convey the information as and when she chose.

So we divided up our corps of spies into a bodyguard, allotting two to each of us, including Chu Chi Ying. They were unarmed, because of the stringent Egyptian law against carrying weapons —a law that, as in every country where it is enforced, works for the crook and against his victim. So they were hardly likely to show much fight in the event of attack; but what they did do was to supply each of us with three pairs of eyes, and to make it fairly safe to sleep for eight hours at a stretch.

Then we examined all the window-shutters, saw to the front-door bolts, barricaded the exit by way of the roof, and filled up everything that would hold water in readiness for an attempt at arson. Finally, Grim collected all our pistols and locked them up in the safe.

"The next stunt brother Zegloush tries will be to tempt us to fire back at somebody," he explained. "If we were fools enough to fire, we'd all be arrested for using firearms; and there's probably influence enough at Zegloush's command to get us deported. If he can deport Joan Angela Leich he'll figure he has the game in his own hands."

We settled down at last for an evening indoors, with the idea of leaving the next move up to the enemy, and Grim took down from the shelf an old copy of Herodotus that he had picked up at a second-hand store. He reads Greek as easily as he could when he left school, which is more than most of us can do, and I shall probably be forgiven for not quoting in the original the paragraph that he finally lighted on after searching the volume for hours. But this was the gist of it:

"Liten," he said quietly. "This is Herodotus describing his travels in Egypt. He is discussing the Great Pyramid and the theory current in his day, that Khufu was buried inside it. He calls Khufu Cheops. 'But the priests told me that Cheops was really buried in a certain place entirely surrounded with water by reason of a conduit that connects it with the River Nile; and where that place is, they said that no man knoweth.'"

"Look, see! Look, see!" chuckled Chu Chi Ying in his corner.

CHAPTER XII
"Damn-fool thinkee money good for dead man. Makee plenty more mistake"

Grim was right as usual. Within the next ten days every trick was tried to tempt us to some act of violence for which we might be arrested. The house next door was an Egyptian's, who lived in part of it and let out the remainder. He turned some tenants out and admitted others for our peculiar annoyance.

They threw things in through our windows, including soaked in oil, and other things that stank. Someone with an air-rifle kept out of sight and potted at whomever he could see between our half-closed shutters. They invaded our roof and set a light to it, and when we went up in a body to extinguish the fire with water-buckets, brickbats and the air-rifle came into use again. It was tempting to hit back, but the temptation was too obvious, especially as Zegloush was known to stand particularly well with the police.

We did not all stay indoors all that time; but, when we walked abroad it was in twos, with our bodyguard on the watch, while the third man kept guard over Chu Chi Ying and the apartment. On two or three occasions our men gave us timely warning of an attempt to rush us in the street; and even Narayan Singh, who is a natural-born fighter, swallowed down his instincts and ran like a rabbit at the very sound of danger. The more we ran away, of course, the more impudent they grew, appreciating that we did, not dare appeal to the authorities.

Nevertheless, what with our alertness and the loyalty of our coloured gang, they hardly did a thousand dollars' worth of damage. A second mob rising that they tried to stir was nipped in the bud by the authorities, and a patrol of British soldiers in an armoured lorry broke up the mob who were busy trying to break in our door on that occasion.

But it reached a point at which the only places where we could be safely seen were the verandas of the big hotels, the racecourse and the clubs, where no attack on us was possible without a clash with the authorities; so when my turn came to venture outdoors I put in more time smoking on the veranda of Shephard's, for instance, than was good for a man of my bulk and active habit. And it was there, on Shephard's veranda, where one half of transient Cairo sits and the other half passes by, that Zegloush Pasha caught sight of me and walked up as friendly as you please. He sat down in the basket-chair beside me and lighted a cigarette, with an air of amusement, before he spoke.

"Well," he said at last, "that was a clever trick you played on me! Oh, yes. Always I admire a man of strategy. Yes, always."

"It's a quality that you and your rascals seem to lack," I answered, and he laughed, but the laugh was superficial; he was one of those fat men who appear good-natured and sportsmanlike on the surface-who, in fact, deliberately cultivate that air; but it was less than skin-deep.

"You have been too clever," he confessed, with a wave of his cigarette and a mock bow. "The worst is that the Chinaman has doubtless told you all he knows. You probably know the value of the secret. That is fine for you, but bad for me! However, the game is not yours quite altogether yet. You realize that, of course?"

He paused for me to answer him; but some of our said-to-be-civilized conventions are not all they are cracked up to be and I chose the way of the untutored savage, saying nothing, moving not a muscle of my face.

"You see," he went on, with the air of a heavy uncle lecturing a spendthrift nephew, "you are a private individual, or perhaps I had better say a number of private individuals—a syndicate, if you prefer it. And you have a secret. But you are vis-a-vis to an organization. You have our political influence to bear in mind. It is true that you have a secret, but it is also true that your secret is valueless-to you, I mean-without the good will of your opponents. Vous comprenez?"

The way to keep out of an argument is not to say anything, so I did exactly that.

"Perhaps you do not understand. You are a stranger. Let me explain. If that secret were to become known to the British authorities, it would be worth nothing to anybody but to them. If there is no law under which they could commandeer everything, they would instantly make one.

They would be very plausible about it, and the law would be made in the public interest-provided that by that I you understand the British public-but they would make the law immediately-at once-and the proclamation would be issued with the ink still wet."

"Whereas, if you had your way?" I suggested.

"There are laws enough," he answered. "The treasure that we know of would find its way into channels where it would do the most good-both politically and to certain individuals of whom you may just as well be one, my friend."

I was not exactly aware of having reached a friendly basis yet; but let that pass.

"What's the great idea?" I asked him.

"Let us be men of business. Before all else, business. I have received a cablegram from a certain Individual, who informs me that you represent the young woman who, by the merest accident, is the present owner of the property in which we are all interested. There are various ways of negotiating this matter. I might say, to commence with, that, as she obtained possession and title while Egypt was under military law, the civil courts can look into the title and perhaps upset it. I have been advised by eminent counsel that there are more improbable contingencies."

"Why don't you go to law then?" I demanded.

"Because, my dear sir, I have proposed that we first talk business. The purpose of business-its legitimate purpose-is to make money. Between men of business the question of price is the paramount consideration. Tell me your price, then, and I will see what can be done."

"My price for what?" I asked him bluntly.

"Well, sir, in the first place, I am suggesting to you that you might advise your principal-this already immensely wealthy young woman-that her legal title to the property in question is so insecure that she would serve her own interest best by accepting a reasonable figure-cash down, of course. And unquestionably, since such advice to her, reasonable though it is, would react to our advantage in certain contingencies, we would expect to compensate you in proportion. That is a sound business principle which my friends and I will gladly recognize."

Well, as a mining engineer, of course, I have had that kind of proposition made to me-less crudely as a rule-at least a score of times. I said nothing, but may have lost control of my face muscles for a second, and he noticed that he had not scored very heavily. So he brought out the next tool from his kit.

"I am told you are a mining man", he resumed. "And of course we shall need a man with great experience of mining to help us in uncovering what we are after, when the time comes, especially as it will be wise to work secretly. So that, if you were to elect to take your compensation in the form of a commission on the proceeds, we are ready to enter into an agreement with you along those lines, as well into an agreement with you along those lines, as well five per cent, what would your idea be as to salary?"

I came back at him with a question:

"When would you propose to start digging?"

"Ah!" he answered. "Your salary as engineer would commence at once. But there are conditions to be considered. Political conditions. Egypt will not remain a British back-garden much longer. When we have control of our own country it will be time enough to begin digging. We would have to wait for the auspicious moment, but you would receive your salary meanwhile, so why should that trouble you? And five per cent of that treasure will certainly amount to an enormous fortune for one individual. Come, let us agree!"

"I'll think it over," I answered.

"I can give you five minutes," he said, pulling out his watch.

"Suppose I don't give you my answer in five minutes?" I asked him.

I'm probably not good at disguising my opinion of a man and his proposals. He changed his tactics instantly, and his manner with them, becoming as deliberately insolent as only an Egyptian can be.

"Miss Leich shall be told the truth, that you have been making overtures for a bribe," he answered. "You are simply a dishonest employee."

I stuck both fists in my pockets from force of habit, for I always do that when I firmly intend not to use them. There were two or three Egyptian officers in dark-blue uniforms keeping a watchful eye from the other end of the veranda, and though it was tempting to take and toss him into the street, that was neither the time nor place. But he mistook the motion, jumped out of his chair, and backed away from me in a great hurry; maybe he had been to the movies and seen Americans using pistols at the least excuse.

As I produced no gun he grew pompously confident again, and went down the steps to the street like a dancing-master, nodding and waving his hand to the police officers with an air of "There you are, my lads; I've turned the trick for you!"

There is a row of shops opposite, and he entered one of them in order to observe the fun through the open door. As soon as he had disappeared inside, one of the police officers —a handsome, swarthy fellow with a saucy upturned moustache-crossed to my end of the veranda and accosted me politely enough.

"Pardon me,' he said, speaking English perfectly. "Have you a pistol in your possession?"

"No."

"Any kind of weapon?"

"No."

"But three of us saw you threaten Zegloush Pasha only a minute ago."

"What do you suggest?" I asked him.

"That you submit to search, effendi."

"By you?"

"Yes."

"All right," I said, "but in the presence of the U.S. Consul. I'll drive there with you, if you care to come."

"Would it not be simpler just to prove to me that you have no weapons?" he asked. "We could step into a nom in the hotel here. It would hardly take a mute."

That sounded reasonable and he spoke with deliberate politeness as if anxious not to appear threatening or insulting. But it is an old game to plant a weapon on a man and then arrest him. Once under arrest, my individual activities in Egypt would be over for some time to come. However, Dame Fortune intervened. One of the assistants from the U.S. Legation drove by that minute, in a hired cab, with a friend. I signalled him.

"Now," I said, "I'll let you search all you want to."

The officer tried to back down then, for he saw that the game was up. But it seemed to me that it was not up. I insisted on being searched.

So we went into the manager's private office and all three police officers went through the farce of searching me, with Lynch, the Legation assistant, looking on. I offered no explanation, so he invited me to lunch, and I drove away with him and his friend, to the disgust of Zegloush, whom I could see peering through the shop door.

Lynch returned to the Legation after lunch, threatening reprisals at police headquarters. The morning hardly seemed to have been wasted.

That night I took the train for Alexandria to meet Mrs. Aintree's boat, Grim having agreed to let me have a try to spike her guns. It seemed well to call her off if that were possible. Any kind of interfering fool might tangle such a complex set of affairs as ours. Nevertheless, my going was a blunder, for all I did was to provide her with an idea that she used against us later.

I explained to Mrs. Aintree that her new husband already had an establishment of wives, and pretended to assume that she would return home on the very next steamer. I even offered to secure accommodation for her.

She laughed.

"Supposing what you say is true, and I have yet to see it proved," she answered, "I am quite able to take care of myself, thank you. I have decided to make Egypt my home."

"Very well," I said, "we're old enemies, but the time is coming when you'll need help, Mrs. Aintree —-"

"Madame Moustapha!" she corrected.

"So remember, Mrs. Aintree, that when you discover, too late, that the U.S. Legation can do nothing for you, my party will be glad to forget old enmities, simply as fellow-countrymen."

It was the unwisest break I ever made. I was talking to a woman who specialized in turning good intentions to her own advantage. She tapped me on the shoulder with the handle of a fly-switch.

"You're bound to be the eventual loser," she assured me. "I'll tell you why. Because you are selfish. You think only of your own pocket, whereas I know what true patriotism means. I am all the time serving' others. This time I am serving Egypt, as you shall see'."

It's no use arguing with anyone who attributes all the vices to you and concedes all the virtues to herself. I took the next train back to Cairo, expecting to be thoroughly laughed at by James Schuyler Grim.

However, he did not laugh. He had been hit by a rock thrown through the window, and, what with headache and my report of failure, was looking on life more gloomily than I had ever known him. Back in the Army-back chancing his neck in the desert country eastward of the Jordan, where, if your life is in your hand, at all events it looks, feels, and tastes of life instead of the fetid, hot streets, that are hardly better than a noisy dream of death to a man who loves the open.

He threw himself back in an armchair and grovelled in pessimism. According to him-and I think he was right at that-the only thing that kept Zegloush and his friends from shooting Atkins out in the desert and seizing Joan Angela's camp by force was fear, not of the courts-for they could fake a strong case for the lawyers easily-but of the small British coterie who still had the upper hand in government. They did not dare arouse the curiosity of those men by calling their attention to that strange well in the desert.

He, Grim, did not dare excite the curiosity of those men either. If information should reach them of the fabulous amount of treasure supposed to be hidden in Khufu's real tomb, that would be the end of Egypt's hope of independence for many a year to come; for, according to Grim, while that fit of blues was on him, no argument except the economic had the slightest force with governments the whole world over, and the real British reason for pulling out of Egypt was simply that it cost too much to stay there.

"And if they stay, there'll be rebellion. If they go, there'll be civil war. Whoever gets that treasure will raise hell with it. Yet it's there, within reach, and it can't be destroyed!"

He dissertated for an hour on local politics, describing the corruption that is part of the very Egyptian atmosphere. He sketched Egyptian history for three thousand years, describing how one conqueror after another has descended on the country, looted and debauched it, and has finally been swallowed and made part of Egypt, ready to lie down and grovel for the next invader.

"Whoever gets those millions can do nothing but raise hell with them!" he repeated.

He described the fellahin-described them in lurid terms-the seemingly passionless bulk of Egypt's population that can rise more swiftly than their mother Nile, and wreak more ghastly devastation, without leaving any fertilizing silt, as the Nile does, by way of compensation after their frenzy has died down again to sullenness. The fellahin, who care for, nothing but their bellies and their buffaloes, and yet who can be whipped up into stark-mad, howling fanaticism by any religious hypocrite with politics up his sleeve-the voters-to-be of Egypt!

"There's bloody murder ahead, whichever way you look!" Grim prophesied.

Then he harped on the string of Joan Angela's coming. She would be assassinated as she stepped ashore. Or, failing that, she would come to Cairo like a typhoon and, in the footsteps of every other moneyed hussy-to quote Grim again-she would try to run things to suit her own crazy notions, would insult the administration, make friends with the wrong people, put the new wine of her absurd ambition into Egypt's ancient bottle, and explode!

"She'll raise hell I tell you. If there's one thing under heaven that's as sure as pay-day, it's that Joan Angela Leich is going to raise insatiable hell!"

Suppose she should get murdered in the streets of Cairo! Setting aside the shame that would be ours in consequence-the black, ingrowing shame of experienced men who have failed their employer-there would then be the United States to reckon with! The Legation would be forced to take it up, and that might lead to international friction.

"As if there weren't enough already!" he groaned.

You can't be a public servant-and the firm of Grim, Ramsden and Ross was that or nothing-without a sense of responsibility. And a sense of responsibility is all right as long as your liver is in first-class working order, but it becomes an overload as soon as pessimism creeps into your veins. Then you can't see the assets for considering the liabilities, and hope, which is driving power in the last analysis, grows cold, fails to expand, and quits. Grim could see all the possibilities of evil in that hour, and not one element of good.

He made the bald, dry statement that there was not one Power in Europe that in the present state of the world's finances would not go to war for the chance of getting hold of Khufu's treasure. Furthermore, that the sum was so vast that no Egyptian politician would hesitate to plunge his country into anarchy in order to get hold of even part of it.

"And if Big Business learns of its existence, Lord help us all!" he grumbled.

He vowed that he could feel the crisis in the air. He swore that Zegloush and his party were only waiting for Joan Angela's arrival in order to play some trump card that would either win them title to the property or give them an excuse for cutting loose with all the forces at their disposal. I suggested that such forces as they might be able to control were only unarmed rabble, whereat he simply snorted with contempt, and quoted G. B. Shaw by the paragraph, word for word, swearing that the our barons, typified by Undershaft and Lazarus, were making up for the business they lost when the Armistice was signed by running cargoes of arms in whole shiploads.

"And d'you suppose their governments are trying to prevent them?" he demanded. "Governments are preventing nothing that can bring in revenue."

He cited instances; gave the names of ships that had been caught in the act of running arms into Egypt from Italy.

"D'you kid yourself they've caught them all?" he asked. "There are rifles and machine-guns cached all over the place!"

He went on to assert that the British force still kept in Egypt was no more than an ably managed bluff. He said there were not enough British troops there to hold the country for a week in the event of a serious uprising, and that all they would attempt to do would be to protect the Suez Canal and keep open the route to India.

"It's a perfect bastard of a proposition!" he complained. "If we took a hundred tons of T.N.T. and blew that Khufu's tomb to atoms, that wouldn't get us anywhere; the money would only be scattered, not destroyed! And it wouldn't be scattered far enough to accomplish anything. It would merely call attention to the stuff, and make it easier to fight for!"

I suggested we might take the bull by the horns and go straight to the Administration with the whole story before Joan Angela's arrival. I did not mean that, and I would have voted against it, but I wanted to switch his thoughts off on to another track and get him into a constructive mood. But I missed my aim.

"Do you suppose there is one man in the Administration who would dare to keep that secret to himself, or any three of them who could keep it between them?" he asked. "The fat 'ud be in the fire within five minutes!"

I asked him what he thought Joan Angela could do, in view of the law about antiquities.

"She can set anarchy loose!" he answered. "She can pull the trigger! Being a woman, she can choose the worst moment for doing it. That's all the difference she can make!"

Narayan Singh was sitting in a shop door opposite, keeping watch on the spies who were watching us. There was nobody else to talk to, so I went upstairs and found Chu Chi Ying as happy as a lunatic among his instruments. He had drawn a great plan of the pyramid, showing an extra chamber right in the middle, about half way between those that were discovered long ago and the apex. He said that it, too, would be discovered one of these days, and I asked him how he knew that.

"Mathlematics no can lie," he answered. "Youu no savvy. Me savvy."

He was obsessed by mathematics; but, according, to him, as I understood his explanations, music and mathematics are the interpretation of law that governs the whole universe, and he who understands them owns the key to everything.

He had that undiscovered chamber in the pyramid all drafted out to scale, showing its exact dimensions and the thickness of its walls. He knew the temperature inside it, or so he declared, saying that it would be found to be midway between the freezing and boiling points of water at that level.

"That one not yet disclovered. When disclovered, same shape-same size-same weight-same sortee stone-all same as Khufu's tomb!"

Nor was that all. He added that Khufu's real tomb would be found at exactly the same distance underground as this undiscovered chamber is above the pyramid foundations.

"Is there anything in that undiscovered chamber?"

Instead of answering he wrote a string of figures on paper, added them, and set down the total.

"Anything in that?" he demanded.

I failed to understand him, so he laughed. I

"Figures-pylamid; same thing!" he explained. "Figures-paper-ink. Pylamid-stone. Same thing! Anything inside pylamid? Same thing inside figures-inside music-nothing. Figures tell something. Music tell something, pylamid tell something."

"According to you, then," I said, "the pyramid is a key to the discovery of Khufu's real tomb. Do you suppose he left any clue as to how that gold could be got out without discovery?"

Chu Chi Ying laughed and rubbed his hands together.

"Khufu think no can do," he answered. "Khufu allee same damn-fool, makee mlistake, not know evlything! Damn-fool thinkee money good for dead man makee plenty more mlistake. Wise man makee look, see. Savee?"

CHAPTER XIII
"Go to it, boys!"

We were all ready for Joan Angela. Two days before her steamer was due word came in from Atkins, out in the desert, that he had succeeded in uncovering a section, ten feet long, of a tunnel built of stone slabs, whose direction corresponded with Chu Chi Ying's rough drawing. With that, Grim's fit of pessimism left him.

We took no chances that could be foreseen, but engaged a suite of rooms for Joan Angela at an hotel in Alexandria and made no stipulation about keeping the reservation secret. We engaged them for a whole week, and paid the money in advance. Then we arranged for a private car to meet her at the docks and convey her straight to the station, where we had a compartment reserved on the Cairo Express in a different name altogether.

Expense being no argument, we repeated that trick in Cairo, reserving rooms for her at one of the but secretly arranging for her to stay as a guest of a banker and his wife, who were friends of Grim's—a Mr. and Mrs. Norwood-people who could be absolutely trusted if it should become necessary to let them into the secret. That arrangement was all the easier to make because Joan Angela had already cabled in advance arranging for credit with the bank of which Norwood was managing director.

The next step was to arrange for Narayan Singh to act as her personal servant and bodyguard. Sikhs, as a rule, do not take kindly to the more menial positions, being by race and religion stalwarts; but Narayan Singh volunteered his services, for his heart was in the game.

Our precautions were not likely to be good for more than a day or two at most, but there is more than a little in keeping the enemy guessing, if only for one day.

It was not likely that they would attempt to murder her at the first start off, because although that might leave them free to begin a lawsuit with her heirs, to upset title to the land, it would certainly compel investigation. The secret of the treasure would then become known to the Administration, which would be the end of its value as far as Zegloush and party were concerned.

But it was perfectly certain that they would discover her whereabouts and start trouble within forty-eight hours at the most; so we laid our plans for action on the very day of her arrival in Cairo. The first move had to be absolutely secret, and Grim took charge of the arrangements for that.

So I met Joan Angela at the dock in Alexandria, and immensely enjoyed the jealousy of sundry British officers, all of whom had laid careful plans for entertaining her. She had come by way of Marseilles, and five days on the P. & O. had been plenty. She had a travelling companion with her, a Mrs. Watts, whom I had never seen or heard of, and they were even making love to that middle-aged, plain, hearty-looking female in order to get the inside track. The unexpected swoop on Cairo took Joan Angela, as well as the enamoured officers, entirely by surprise, for we had been careful in the wireless that we sent her to mention no more than that the suite had been reserved at the Alexandria hotel.

My job, until we reached Cairo, was to persuade Joan Angela and Mrs. Watts of the seriousness of the situation, and I might just as well have tried to persuade two gobs off a warship that the shore police should be considered with respect. It wasn't possible, and that was all about it. They would take nothing seriously, not even my warning that their lives were in danger. Exuberant animal spirits was the diagnosis, and I had no physic that would fit the case.

Joan Angela had reached her own conclusions; and since arguing with a woman who has done that always seems to me an even more futile and irritating waste of time than golf or tiddly-winks, I gave it up at last, and laughed with them.

We arrived in Cairo long after dark, and there Grim met us, with Narayan Singh looming behind him like a jinnee out of the Arabian Nights. He had a great hired limousine in waiting, and took us straight to the hotel instead of to the Norwoods' house. There Mrs. Watts was installed in the suite we had reserved for Joan Angela, and thither came Norwood presently, with his own private car, in a hurry to carry his guest away. But he had to wait, for Grim had worked a miracle.

There were two men in Egypt at that moment who really ranked as statesmen, and nobody quite knew which of them held the reins in the absence of the High Commissioner. Theoretically they were members of a council; but as there never yet was a theory that could be confined within four walls, nor a council that functioned as intended, those two men notoriously held control between them. Needless to say, they were perfectly aware of it. And if you think it is simple to persuade such men to come to you and hear your story, instead of your going to them and waiting on their convenience, just try it once and see. Grim had persuaded both those men to come to the hotel and listen to what we had to say; and said miracle gave birth to a young one en route, for they kept their appointment to the minute.

Simultaneously with them arrived Chu Chi Ying, blinking through horn-rimmed spectacles, holding great rolls of drawings in his hand, and bowing to everybody like one of those toy mandarins whose heads are balanced on a pendulum.

The financial member of a council always considers himself the most important. Like the other, the legal member, this one was a Scotsman-a short, full-tummied, grey, nearly bald man of about sixty, who bowed to Joan Angela, sat down with his hands folded one on top of the other on his lap, and studied Joan through his gold-rimmed spectacles. He was suspicious of her, having daughters of his own, nevertheless respectful, because in his estimation money was the life-blood of civilization.

The other man was rather tall and lean and canny-looking-decidedly inclined to be flirtatious in a noncommittal way; he somehow conveyed the impression of holding a power-of-attorney empowering him to flirt on behalf of the British nation, and of being careful not to let the nation go too far.

Like most middle-aged family-men they were half scandalized and half captured by Joan Angela's good looks. Nevertheless, first, last, and all the time they were on their guard lest some trick might be played on the Government they represented.

Grim opened the ball without preliminary. He told the whole story of the effort to form an incorporation in the U.S. in order to get title to the thousand acres in the Fayoum and exploit them under the aegis of the U.S. Government. Then he described our adventure in rescuing Chu Chi Ying out of the empty house next door to that occupied by Zegloush Pasha.

"You broke the law there!" snapped the legal member, pursing up his lips.

Grim did not wait for any dissertation on the legal aspects of the situation, but promptly tackled Chu Chi Ying's deductions from the pyramid, hitting only the high places, so to speak, and merely tracing the outline of how the calculations indicated that strange well in the desert, and how we had investigated it, and what we had discovered there.

Both members of the council looked incredulous. The legal member curled his lip, and the two men exchanged glances of derision that I suppose they thought we were too bat-blind to notice. Joan Angela was taking particular notice of everything, however, and said nothing.

Grim, who felt the coolness with which his statements were received, sat down and asked Chu Chi Ying to show his map and diagrams. Nothing could have pleased the old Chinaman better; he started to spread them out on the floor, perhaps thinking that the members of the council would squat on the carpet beside him and be entertained. But there was nothing of that sort going to happen.

"We've all heard a very great deal of nonsense talked about the Great Pyramid," said the legal member. "There are theories and theories about it, but few of them are even plausible to my way of thinking. I have even gone so far as to read one or two books that have been published in order to prove that the pyramid sets the date for the end of the world. All very ridiculous, I think. The pyramid was a tomb-just a tomb and nothing else. As for that well in the desert-it may possibly be in some way connected with another tomb; but it seems to me that you have let yourselves be carried away by-ah-cacoethes antiquarii."

The financial member, with his hands still folded in his lap and his spectacles down on the end of his nose, nodded and smiled.

"Cacoethes antiquarii is a disease rather prevalent in Egypt. It's endemic," he said dryly.

"Do you think I have it?" asked Joan Angela quietly.

She was looking straight at the financial member; he could not avoid her eyes, and I don't think he wanted to, although he found her silk stockings almost equally attractive.

"You seem to me to have come a very long way to investigate a mare's nest," he said with a little apologetic laugh.

"It's my property. Can anybody stop my digging there?" she asked.

"No," replied the legal member. "You may dig on your own land."

"And keep any treasure I find?"

"Ah! That's different. If you should discover a gold mine, you could work it, I believe. There are so few mines here that I'm not familiar with the regulations. I can inquire, if you wish."

"I asked about treasure-gold or silver bullion-ornaments-coin-that kind of thing."

"That would not be yours. Treasure of that sort would have to be surrendered. If it had no particular intrinsic value you might be permitted to export portions of it, but not otherwise."

"What sort of man is this Zegloush Pasha?" she asked next, switching her line of attack. Both men were perfectly aware she was attacking. They made wry faces, and glanced at each other again.

"I advise you to have nothing whatever to do' with him," said the financial member "He is a politician of the meanest calibre, who enjoys an unsavoury reputation. Enjoys it, I said."

"Would you prefer to deal with him or with me?" she asked instantly. "I could sell the property to-night to Zegloush and his friends. Would you I like me to do that?"

"Why not sell it back to the Government?" suggested the legal member.

But the financial member shook his head.

"No funds!" he remarked with an air of finality.

"I propose to reach a decision this evening," said Joan Angela, and both members of the council raised their eyebrows in alarm. They were not used to dealing with young women who stood right up to them.

"All the way down from Alexandria," she continued, "I've been listening to a sermon from Mr. Ramsden about the danger if Zegloush should get hold of the treasure that's supposed to be in Khufu's tomb."

"Nothing could be worse!" said the financial member.

"Nothing!" agreed the other.

"Very well," said Joan Angela. "If you ask me not to sell to Zegloush Pasha —"

"I have advised you to have nothing whatever to do with Zegloush," said the financial member.

"Thank you for advice," Joan answered, "but you'll have to do more than advise. If you don't want me to sell —"

"Please don't," said the financial member.

"Very well," she answered. "But who is to have that treasure, supposing it's there?"

"We would like time to consider that," said the legal member.

"We have until midnight," she answered sweetly.

"We could only discuss the question unofficially, then."

"Go ahead," she answered. "Be as unofficial as you please. Who does that treasure rightfully belong to, if it's there?"

"To the Government," said the legal member.

"Which Government?" she asked. "The Egyptian Administration?"

Both men hesitated palpably.

"The Egyptian Administration," said the lawyer, "is in a peculiar, I might say unique, position. You might say we are trustees, holding Egypt on behalf of her foreign creditors, who are of almost every race under the sun. That was the original condition of occupation, and the change from avowed protectorate to decidedly qualified independence has hardly changed that. So, legally speaking, I would have to answer your question, perhaps, in one way; ethically, in another."

"You might dig out that treasure and hand it over to the Egyptian politicians to spend," she suggested. "Perhaps they would pay Egypt's debts with it,"

"Perhaps!" the financial member remarked dryly.

"You have raised a fine point," said the legal member, setting the tips of his fingers together and crossing his legs. "Supposing the treasure to be there, and if we were to say for the sake of argument that it belongs to the latter-day Egyptians because a king who reigned four thousand years ago raised the money in the form of taxes, we would be assuming what we cannot prove, On the same basis you would have to assume that buried treasure discovered, say, in Mexico belonged exclusively to the descendants of the Aztecs. But suppose we listen first to you, Miss Leich; you must have had some definite idea before coming all this distance. We are speaking unofficially, remember."

Joan Angela smiled, and I knew that minute she had made her mind up, and had only waited to be asked to state her terms.

"That money belongs to the whole world," she answered. Her voice was in the middle of the note, and her mind in the middle of the track. She was speaking from conviction, saying something that was as clear to her as twice two equals four.

"That's an original suggestion!" said the legal member.

"Original, very!" the other echoed.

"I've no objection to the British being trustees for it," Joan Angela went on. "I think they're entitled to be. Fifty years ago Egypt was a desert; everybody knows that. To-day it's a rich country, and Egyptians have done precious little in return, except to swindle foreigners. If there really is treasure in Khufu's tomb, I reckon Egypt owes it to the world!"

"Original! Original! Then what do you propose?" asked the financial member.

"To dig! We'll soon know whether it's there or not. If it is, I want it used in the general public interest, in the form of a trust, and I want a vote on the board of trustees. If you'll agree to that, all right. If not, I'll sell the land to the highest bidder and let the future take care of itself."

"My dear lady, we have no authority to treat with you in a matter of that kind!" exclaimed the legal member.

"You're men, aren't you?" she retorted. "If you don't agree, you can say so."

"We'll have to think it over."

"You've until midnight," she answered.

"But arrangements would have to be made to keep any such solution absolutely secret in order to avoid an uprising, and how can that be done, if, as you say, Zegloush and his party already know of the existence of the treasure?" objected the legal member.

"You can leave that to my gang," she answered. "They're a good gang. If they get any kind of square deal from you folks there's nobody on earth can beat them."

"You mean you want the British Government to have that money?" asked the financial member, looking at her in amazement over the top of his spectacles.

"On trust, and for a public purpose," she retorted. "If I thought you'd pay your war-debts with it, I'd say take it, but I don't believe your alleged statesmen 'ud do that. They'd start a new war. If I find the treasure on my land and let you British have it, it's to go to a board of trustees-gentlemen, not politicians."

"We can't pledge the British Government, you know!"

"Nobody can. Your politicos are as rotten as ours in the U.S. But you've some gentlemen, haven't you, outside politics?"

The financial member sat back and chuckled. The legal member stared. Norwood, the banker, walked across the room and chose another chair. Grim turned round to hide a smile and avoided looking at me for fear I would wink at him. The financial and the legal member exchanged glances.

"Very well," said the financial member, rising. "In our private capacity, speaking strictly unofficially, we agree to do our best toward that solution, if the treasure is there."

Joan Angela gave him no opportunity to hedge on that.

"Good! Go to it, boys!" she said, smiling at I Grim and me. "Good night, all! I won't keep Mr. Norwood waiting any longer."

CHAPTER XIV
"Please come quickly!"

Joan Angela awfully resented having Narayan Singh dancing constant attendance on her. But Norwood and his wife were equally relieved, for it is no joke having a millionairess in your house with an Egyptian feud against her. Mrs. Watts occupied Joan's suite at the hotel, and Joan was spirited away near midnight in a closed car, but Zegloush knew before morning where she was staying. Narayan Singh, surveying the world at large before breakfast, recognized the same old street-cleaner spy and his assistant who had hitherto loafed in our street and reported our doings.

So when we called with a car to take her to view the property, that move was known to the enemy at once. Luckily they did not know of our interview with two members of the council, both of whom had left by a back way after midnight, provided with perfect alibis by Grim, who leaves as little to Lady Luck as can be managed.

Have you ever seen a map of the Fayoum? It is an extraordinary section of flat country that was once a lake-bed. In places where water reaches it the soil is immensely fertile, and every yard of that is cultivated by the peasantry, who live in the usual stinking Egyptian villages among their hens and thriving insects. But the edge of the Fayoum is not at all regular, so that the desert crowds it much as a sand-beach holds back the sea, in curves and promontories, and wherever, for any reason, the irrigation stops short, there the desert encroaches.

Joan Angela's thousand acres were unquestionable desert on a promontory jutting into the Fayoum, so that within a few miles there were half a dozen filthy villages, containing on the average two or three hundred inhabitants apiece, scattered southward and south-eastward in an uneven semicircle. Toward the south west all was sand as far as the distant limestone hills.

We started with the road to ourselves, except for peasantry bringing in their market stuff, but we began to be followed before long by two of those gorgeously painted, brazenly-trumpeting, sport-model cars in which the soul of the moneyed Egyptian delights. They kept behind us until, we left the avenue of lebbakh trees and the pyramid, and turned off into the desert. Then, though, they put on speed and passed, taking a line at an angle to ours, sufficiently close to us as they went by to disclose the fact that the leading car was driven by Zegloush himself. He turned his head to grin in our direction, and was evidently pleased that we should recognize him.

Two of the men in the car behind were the identical police officers who had searched me in Shepheard's Hotel, although on this occasion they were not in uniform; they even went so far as to raise their hands in a sort of mock salute, and if anything in the world was obvious it was that they were bent on mischief and equally bent on our knowing that they, and none others, were responsible for what was going to happen.

As we had no weapons it would have been wise to return to Cairo, but Joan Angela would not hear of it. She said that coloured men were no more difficult to face than whites. You can't argue with a woman when she owns millions, and you like her, and she sees, or thinks she sees a chance to benefit the wide world, so forward we went, losing sight of all except the dust of those other cars long before we reached Joan's camp and found Atkins and his staff busy with their excavation.

They had uncovered about twenty feet of what I looked like pavement, constructed of huge stone slabs, but it was much too wide to be a water- conduit, although Atkins swore he could hear water gurgling underneath. We slid down the sand to the bottom and listened, but could hear nothing, and Chu Chi Ying shook his head. He said it was too far to the southward by at least fifty yards, and not nearly deep enough below the desert level. Atkins had been trying to pry up one of the stones I with the meagre means at his disposal, but they must have weighed thirty or forty tons apiece.

On Chu Chi Ying's advice we staked out another sand-patch, seventy-five yards south, and told Atkins to pitch another marquee and dig there, promising to send him out a good gang with plenty of tools the next day. He went about pitching the marquee at once; but before his men had dragged the heavy canvas out from one of the wooden huts we learned what Zegloush and his friends had gone for.

Warning came from the direction of the distant villages-sudden tumult-several hundred men advancing, roaring like a tidal wave and throwing up the sand in handfuls as they rushed. Their dust was like a battle-squadron's smoke-screen. You could only see the sticks they carried brandishing above the cloud. But you could recognize their roar; there was no mistaking it-the very worst mob war-cry that there is.

"La allah ilia Allah! La allah ilia Allah!"

Get those sullen, stolid fellahin once shouting their blind creed in unison, and after that about the only argument worth using on them is machine-guns. There was no room for doubt as to which way they were coming, or what their business was; they were headed our way, and the business was to beat us with their long sticks into red mud that would by and by cockle in the heat and go blowing downwind, leaving broken bones for the jackals to come and crack.

"I'll bet you he's been telling them," said Grim, "that we're here to lower the price of cotton in some ingenious way. Well-all aboard! Atkins, you and your gang had better climb on the running-board. We'll pull our freight out ahead of them."

That was perfectly sound tactics. It was even possible that by driving slowly and keeping well in sight of the mob we might draw them away from the camp and save the wooden buildings from destruction. We were going to need those buildings to house labourers. Grim took the wheel, and instead of retreating made a circuit in the mob's direction, merely keeping out of range of sticks and stones.

We headed eastward and they changed direction, swooping after us. If there had ever been a doubt of their intention, there was none now. The fellah would always rather kill than burn; centuries of the kourbash under the rule of conquerors have taught him that violence should be applied to persons; he will kill, when aroused, with a ferocity that surpasses the ravening of animals, but, unlike folk who are a fraction less materially minded, prefers not to destroy what he would rather tear down and steal at his leisure.

So it began to look like a mere amusing interlude, for they had no chance of catching us. We kept just sufficiently far ahead of them to draw them away from the camp. We were all laughing, when something went suddenly wrong with the engine; it heated up, the radiator boiled over, and we stopped. The mob yelled. Grim got the engine going again, but only for about a minute, and the second time we stopped the fellahin realized that we were in serious difficulty. Atkins got down and jerked up the engine-cover, and Grim and I climbed out. The roar that went up from the fellahin about three hundred yards away was the voice of ancient Egypt, as merciless as her scorpions and her sun-baked sky.

"Damn bad pigeon!" remarked Chu Chi Ying, folding his arms on the mid-ship seat philosophically.

There was no time to discover what the trouble was. Atkins lined up his little party of drilled automatons and told them to wrench sticks away from the mob. Grim and I got the tools out, and made shift to do our utmost with a hammer and a wrench, passing to Atkins the short iron bar that belonged to the jack, and I dare say that between us we might have done some damage before the end came-especially as Narayan Singh contrived to tear loose the iron foot-rest from the floor of the car: given any kind of weapon, he was sure to kill half a dozen men before they overwhelmed him. Joan Angela got out of the car and stood behind me.

"I'll take your hammer when you're down," she I said quietly.

The mob was not fifty yards away, and a stone or two had come whizzing in our direction, when Zegloush and the two cars appeared from behind the dust-cloud, charging through the mob, knocking them right and left and getting between the raging fanatics and us. The plainclothes police officers had revolvers and used them, firing in the air, and the others stood up, waving their arms, shouting, haranguing.

The mob checked sullenly-Egypt harking to the voice of her oppressors. But even so, nine or ten of them sprinted by and closed with us. We had our work cut out for a minute or two, for if you want to layout the angry fellah without killing him you've a scuffle on your hands. But, exactly as the hot wind dies after stirring up the desert into dusty hell, the mob grew sullen and submissive-not reasonable, you understand: it simply quit-ceased shouting, ceased throwing up the sand, and stood looking on possessed by a sort of contemptuous curiosity, and reeking to high heaven from the sweat on its filthy cotton clothing. That's Egypt, sullen and fanatically fierce by turns-five thousand years of unmodified heredity, obedient to its robber-pasha, as it always has been, saying "Kismet! The pasha is the will of God!"

Within five minutes, lashed by the tongue of Zegloush and his friends, they were off back to their villages at a dog-trot, pursued by the nine or ten whom we had bruised with our improvised weapons, and Zegloush drove up, smiling like a papier-mache Turk, to inquire whether anyone was hurt. He introduced himself to Joan Angela.

"I am Zegloush Pasha. Are you Miss Leich? I am glad to make your acquaintance. You are fortunate to make mine! I have saved your life, and if you are wise you will save yourself some serious trouble by listening to me. Those friends of yours are not well qualified to advise you, for they don't understand conditions. You have seen this morning what will happen if you try to excavate on that land that you are supposed to own. The fellahin resent interference by foreigners. Besides, your title to that land is very insecure, to say the least of it, so the best thing you can do is to sell it to me, for I understand these villagers and can manage them. I will pay you a reasonable price."

He was radiantly confident-beaming with self admiration-perfectly sure that we were now amenable-and sweating from his exhortation to the mob. The police in the car behind him were grinning like thieves who have got away with something.

"I'm not in the least afraid of your mob," Joan Angela answered.

Grim and I were working at the engine; all that was wrong was a broken water-connection, which was easy enough to fix, and we had plenty more water in a goat-skin bag.

"If you think you can frighten me, summon them back!"

His tarboosh nearly fell off with astonishment.

"My mob? What do you mean-my mob?" he demanded.

"They came and went at your bidding," she answered.

His fat face darkened, and he showed his teeth in a venomous grin. "Ah! You think you are very clever, Miss American High-life," he sneered. "However, you shall see!"

He drove off without another word, straight toward Cairo, putting on speed at risk to his expensive springs; and when we had fixed the broken joint with a piece of rubber piping, and had refilled the radiator, we returned to the camp, none of us, I think, feeling particularly confident except Joan Angela.

"If I die for it, I'll take care that that creature doesn't have his way," she said quietly.

But Grim took her in hand then, in the little hot camp-office that Atkins had converted into quarters for himself, and a lecture from Grim carries absolute conviction. He assured her that we were all ready to see the venture through, but that the life of every one of us, hers included, was worth less than a day's purchase unless she watched her step. He likened Egypt to a desert full of unseen cobras that strike without warning, and insisted above all else that she should take utmost advantage of Narayan Singh's willingness to be her bodyguard.

That part rankled. She had no objection personally to Narayan Singh, but she was too well used to her own way to be shepherded by anyone. The frankness and readiness to meet anyone face to face that were her best possible protection in a civilized land were hardly a protection against folk who don't admire that kind of thing; but it was hard to make her see that.

Another difficulty was that Narayan Singh, being a Sikh, was well aware of the usual attitude of white toward the dark-whatever the dark man's creed or quality. He would not over-assert himself. His own self-respect would prevent him from chancing a rebuke, and it was likely to be easy for her to give him the slip if that was her intention. Grim urged her to make it her business to keep the Sikh within sight or reach.

She promised, and she meant it, but habit is too hard to be overcome by a fifteen-minute lecture, even when Grim does the persuading, and I took Narayan Singh aside.

"If she won't listen, compel her!" I said. "'I'm with you, if there's trouble afterwards."

He laughed.

"You and I are friends, sahib. I could take you by the throat and choke you into submission, if that were the only way, and no harm done. You could strike me, if I were mad and would not listen, and I would thank you for it afterwards. But with Miss Leich it is otherwise. She may strike me, if she wishes. If she gives an order, I shall obey. My life is at her service, I having pledged it. But I will lay no hand on her."

He was near enough right in his attitude to be proof against any argument of mine, and we had nobody else we could trust to protect her and who at the same time could act the part of household servant at the Norwoods' without exciting comment, so there was nothing for it but to trust Dame Fortune-an untrustworthy jade. We drove back to Cairo, and arrived there probably three hours later than Zegloush and his party, well along in the afternoon; and three hours is a lot of time to allow to a mischievous, ambitious rascal who has influence, besides being plenty long enough for the impression made by a lecture to wear or.

We picked up Mrs. Watts at the hotel, and drove her and Joan Angela to the Norwoods' house, where we left Narayan Singh on guard. Then we returned to our own quarters to make arrangements for a labour gang, and Grim went off to interview the financial member of the council, to see whether he couldn't arrange for British soldiers to be quartered at the camp as a precaution against further interference by the villagers. So I was all alone when, just about six o'clock in the evening, there began to be another of those swiftly rising, savage riots for which Cairo was always famous-riots that explain why there is always at least one British regiment under arms in the Citadel.

It was a savage riot this time, as fierce as it was sudden-one of thirty that took place that year. The demagogues out of office were keeping the crowd stirred up, on the time-worn principle, or lack of it, that the political fishing is easiest in troubled waters. They called this particular thing a bread riot. Bread was the same price as usual, and the bakers were earning less than usual, but it suited somebody to have a riot, so the bakers had to suffer.

Suffer they did, for the military could not protect them all at a moment's notice. It had been known at headquarters for days past that a riot might break out at any time, but nobody had been able to foresee on whose helpless necks the fury of fend himself would do for a scapegoat. The mob was sore, and all the politicians had to do was to direct its insane anger at somebody. They picked on the bakers as the easiest mark in sight, an appeal to the belly being irresistible.

So up the streets the mob came howling, breaking in the bakers' windows and plundering on their way, with lorries full of soldiers and machine-guns in hot pursuit-all arms loaded with blank for the present, as the mob knew perfectly.

From out of my window I saw them drag one wretched Armenian baker from his cart, in which he had the loaves piled for his evening trade, beat him almost unconscious, drag him through his open shop door, and hurl him into his oven to bake to death. His screaming wife tried to drag the door open, so they hurled her in after him, and the British soldiers forced their way on the scene too late to do more than break a head or two with their rifle-butts and rescue two charred corpses. So far the soldiers had not fired a shot or used a bayonet, although most of them were bleeding. The butt and boot were the gist of their argument, and the mob was using anything within reach.

In the midst of all that came Narayan Singh, three steps at a stride upstairs, bursting in, breathless. He said nothing, but his eyes looked wild, and he thrust forward a crumpled letter for me to read. There wasn't much he could say in the circumstances. The letter ran:

Dear Miss Leich,

Please pardon my approaching you. I am in dreadful trouble. I recently married in America a Pasha who now turns out to have an establishment of three wives, all under one roof. He has my money. I have lost my citizenship and am helpless. He is ill-treating me, and I don't know to whom to turn unless to you, in the hope that your generosity will send you to my aid. I am ill and unable to walk; I am not sure I have not been poisoned; but my tormentor is away from home at the moment, and if you could come and carry me away to some safe place I would be everlastingly grateful. The servants would admit a woman into the house, but they would be afraid to admit you if you had an escort, so please don't think of bringing any men-folk, for that would mean the end of me. Bring another woman if you like. This servant, who, I think, is faithful, has orders to use my last remaining money to hire a carriage and bring you here, if you will come. Please come quickly. I know that if you don't I shah be dead within a day or so. If you will come I will tell you the whole secret of your land in the Fayoum. I am vomiting. I think it is arsenic. Oh, do, please, come quickly! You knew me as-Isabel Aintree.

It was blank paper, undated, no address.

"Did she go?" I demanded.

"Sahib, I—"

"Did she go alone?"

"Nay, I prevented that. She took the other mem-sahib. There came this black brute of a servant, looking more sly than a fox around the hen-yard, and I met him at the door. He gave me this letter for the mem-sahib, so I delivered it; and she, having read it in a moment, said that she would go, whereat I made ready to go with her. But she said no, there must be no man with her, and I, remembering your words, sahib, declared with much determination that she shall not go unaccompanied. Whereat she laughed and said the other mem-sahib shall go with her, for two women, said she, are the equal of one man at all times. And I still expostulating, she gave me a positive order, which I could not help but obey. She bade me bring this letter to you, sahib, saying that the letter itself explains all, and that you will surely understand. What little else there was to do I did. I demanded of the driver whence he came and whither he was going. He mumbled words that I could not hear, until both memsahibs were inside the carriage, and then spat at me and drove on. The carriage had no name or number on it. So the two mem-sahibs are gone, and we are men without honour."

"Could you recognize the driver, or the servant who gave you the letter, if you saw them again?" I asked.

"Try me, sahib! I have a score to settle with both of them!"

The telephone wasn't working. It almost never does when a mob cuts loose. There was no way of getting in touch with Grim, and there wasn't much sense in wasting twenty minutes going to the Norwoods' house. All I could think of was Will Tryon back there in California, faithful and straight as one of those great pine-trees, counting implicitly me to send his young employer safely home again. I seemed to see Will Tryon's face between me and the wall whichever way I looked. It wasn't any use cursing old King Khufu and his treasure; that would cut no ice with Will Tryon. If I ever wanted to look that fellow in the face again, I had got to do the right thing now, and do it quick.

I thought of the police. They were on riot duty. Whoever was left at headquarters would laugh. If he were asked to find a missing woman out of hand, especially as the carriage in which she drove away had no number on it. I thought of government headquarters and the military, but exactly the same argument applied. They would find her, certainly-dead, possibly-within the week, probably. I needed to find her now, within the hour.

I thought of hurrying to the residence of Zegloush Pasha and kicking in the door, for you get wild notions in such moments; but the certainty that he would have me arrested for taking part in the riot cut short the drift of that idea. The one paramount question was how to discover exactly where Joan Angela was gone; after that would be the time to take chances. But the streets were full of men about as reasonable as mad dogs. The police and military were only gradually getting the upper hand and driving folk within doors. There was the certainty of being turned over to the military-who lock you up first and ask questions tomorrow-if I should fall foul of Zegloush before knowing Joan Angela's whereabouts for certain. And Narayan Singh stood looking at me, miserably humble, self-condemned for having let her out of sight; there was not a chance of getting an idea from him.

I don't believe Joan Angela would have been alive today if it had not been for Chu Chi Ying. I would most likely have dashed out into the street with the Sikh at my heels, and Lord knows what form failure would have taken. Only I should have failed; that is outside the pale of argument. But as the Sikh and I stood there, reading baffled irresolution in each other's eyes, old Chu Chi Ying came downstairs smiling blandly, to ask what the noise in the street was all about.

He was the last man in the world you would naturally ask advice from in a crisis; but he could recognize a crisis as quickly as anyone, and he stood still for about a minute in the doorway, blinking at the two of us.

"No can do?" he asked, as if we had been "fat-fool first mates" in a quandary over some theoretical navigation question he had set for us.

I had to say something, ask something, confer with somebody, or bust. I dare say you know the feeling. It makes It makes us take the most unlikely people into confidence.

"Did you tell your story to anyone else, than Zegloush Pasha?" I asked the old Chinaman.

He blinked, and seemed to swallow his Adam's apple.

"Heap plenty men," he answered.

"Where? In his house?"

He shook his head.

"This miserable Chinaman, he receive much hospitality at first. Many people paying compliments. Much how-de-do."

"But was all this in Zegloush Pasha's house? That's what I'm driving at."

He shook his head again.

"Taking this miserable Chinaman there afterwards. Much plomise before going. After get there, no can do!"

"All right. Where was the house where you did the talking?"

"In Clairo," he answered, wrinkling his forehead.

"Could you find it again?"

"Mebbe."

"What sort of house was it?"

"Plivate house."

"Full? Empty? Big? Little? Where was it?"

"Yes," he answered, blinking and looking preternaturally wise.

"Infidel!" snarled Narayan Singh, taking a stride toward him. "I am a man of blood, as you have called me many times. I am bellicose. Answer the sahib's question!"

"Big house, little street, little doorway, full that time, empty by and by," said Chu Chi Ying quickly, as if he were reeling off an exorcism.

"Was there anyone there whom you could recognize besides Zegloush?" I asked him.

"Zegloush heap plenty fliends."

"Would you know any of them again?"

He wrinkled his forehead in a sort of criss-cross question mark.

"Can find house. Can happen," he said doubtfully.

"Let's go!" said I. "Wrap him up and carry him, Narayan Singh!"

My brain was working at last. It balks like a mule at the wrong time always; but just once so often I get the right idea, and then my thews and sinews take charge and something happens. Narayan Singh, whose greatest quality is swift obedience, snatched one of Grim's Bedouin cloaks from a hook behind the door, caught the protesting Chinaman in its folds like a fish in a net, and picked him up as if he were a baby.

"Come on!"

We shot downstairs and into the street as if the house were on fire, poor old Chu Chi Ying suffering uncomplainingly as his legs hit the corners, and at the foot of the stairs we cannoned into Grim.

"Come on!" I answered.

So we took the sidewalk at a run together, and before we had gone half a block an officer called from a passing armoured lorry to know what we had there, and where we were bound.

"Wounded man!" I shouted.

"All right," he answered. "Get indoors as quick as possible, and stay there."

The principle was to get all Europeans off the streets. We were stopped six times in half a mile by officers, some of whom insisted on seeing our 'wounded man'. But by that time Chu Chi Ying had the rules of the game down fine, and when an officer uncovered him he rolled his eyes, stuck out his tongue, and made such grimaces that he almost convinced me. Between times he directed us from street to street, and I told Grim briefly what had happened.

"It was my fault!" growled Narayan Singh, crushing Chu Chi Ying so savagely that the Chinaman yelled. "1 will never forgive myself."

"If you talk rot I'll give you no chance to redeem yourself!" Grim retorted. "Have you never seen me make mistakes?"

That was the last word, so far as I know, that was ever exchanged between them on that subject, but it had a bearing on what followed, for a Sikh, like most other men, reacts gratefully to that kind of treatment.

The street fighting was by no means over, although most of the whites were safe indoors and the men in uniform were in such strong detachments that they were having matters their own way. But, when the lorries passed, the fighting resumed down the side streets behind them, for there's no time like a riot for paying off old scores, and in Egypt — Cairo especially-everybody has a grudge against almost everybody else. The ambulances were scooting like hawks along a hedgerow, and every once in a while a shot would ring out to remind the crowds that the machine-guns were ready for business.

Narayan Singh would not let either of us carry e Chinaman. He liked the effort. He was doing penance. Chu Chi Ying weighed less than a hundred pounds, but did you ever try to carry that much in your arms at a good, sharp trot? The Sikh never set his burden down once, nor paused to shift it; and he seemed to be going as strong as ever when, under Chu Chi Ying's direction, we turned down a narrow alley between high walls. There were trees peering over the top of the walls in places, but that was only in between high buildings, whose windows were small, high up, and barred with iron.

All down that street there was only one doorway, and that hardly more than a slit in the high wall. The wall was built of limestone looted from ancient monuments-as likely as not from the casing of the Great Pyramid —and the door was of iron, set deep in mortice, so that neither locks nor hinges were visible from outside.

"There! That door!" said Chu Chi Ying, and the Sikh set him on his feet at last.

Without a word Grim took to his heels and ran straight on down the alley at full pelt. I was just in time to see an Egyptian in tarboosh and patent leather shoes disappear round the corner into another alley that crossed ours nearly at right angles, but as Grim can run about two yards to my one I did not join in the pursuit. Instead, I began examining the iron door, wondering how we could get inside it.

It was Narayan Singh, Sikh-fashion observing everything with hardly a motion of his head, who, saw and pounced on incontestable evidence that we had come to the right place. He picked up a piece of extremely fine linen about an inch, and a half square that lay between the cobble-stones to one side of the door, and passed it to me.

"Does the sahib recognize that?"

It had been torn from Joan Angela Leich's handkerchief. There was no doubt of it. It bore the initials J. A. L. done in a peculiar style of needle work. The linen might have come from almost any expensive store, but that peculiar embroidery was done by a Piute Indian at only one place in the world. Nor had the scrap of linen been wrenched off in a scuffle. It was torn off square, deliberately.

CHAPTER XV
"Speak, o man of swift decisions!"

Grim came back, dragging the Egyptian with him —a sulky, well-dressed, pimply-faced, obvious debauchee, who swore by Allah he would have Grim punished. He denied ever having been through that iron door; denied even knowing whose house it belonged to. But Chu Chi Ying identified him as one of the men who had been in the house when he first told his story of Khufu's real tomb to a committee of Zegloush Pasha's friends.

"I never saw that Japanese in my whole life!" the Egyptian protested.

"Kill um dead!" suggested our Chinese friend.

Narayan Singh went in search of a crowbar, but might as well have looked for diamonds.

Grim offered to let the Egyptian go if he would tell where Joan Angela Leich and Mrs. Watts were at that minute.

"Hasn't there been a riot?" he retorted. "What stupidity to ask me! Rioters have certainly seized them and carried them off! Quelle betise! Je m'en fiche de vos dames americaines. Women who accept invitations to ride in strange carriages deserve whatever happens to them!"

That was not convincing. Narayan Singh, returning from a fruitless hunt, tried other tactics.

"Do you want to die, Egyptian?" he demanded.

"Dog of an Indian!"

The Sikh grinned. He dared kill anyone that minute. But Grim shook his head, and then turned suddenly. Back at the corner of the alley behind us an armoured lorry had come to a standstill while its youthful officer made up his mind which street to patrol next. Grim passed the Egyptian to me to hold, and again went off at a run. In a minute he was talking to the officer. In another minute the officer and ten privates had climbed down from the lorry, leaving only two men in charge, and were following Grim in our direction.

"Miss Leich and Mrs. Watts are in here through that door?" asked the officer, nodding to me; and I recognized him for one of the gallants who had been so disappointed when I carried Joan Angela off from under his guns, so to speak, in Alexandria. He was a clean young fellow, with a campaign scar across his cheek.

"I don't dare break that door down. By God, you know, they'd break me for it."

"If the door were open would you follow through?" Grim asked him.

"I'll set a guard over it, if you like, while we pass the buck to somebody and get permission to break in."

But I decided on a swifter method. I took that Egyptian by the throat and hurled him against the iron door backward so hard that some of his false teeth fell out.

"You open that," I said, "or I'll kick you through it!"

I meant it. He knew I meant it. If he hadn't the means of opening that door, so much the worse for him. He hesitated, so I gave him another dose of the same medicine, and he made up what was left of his mind that of two evils his Egyptian friends were probably less dangerous.

"That is enough!" he stammered. "I open presently! Just wait!"

I conceded him one minute. He took a clasp-knife from his pocket and rapped out a signal on the iron. It was repeated after a moment from within. He rapped out another signal. We heard a heavy bar being shifted, and the door swung open about six inches, which was plenty in the circumstances. The lot of us went through like a winning football team, into a garden full of grapes and gorgeous flowers, with date-palms spaced at intervals. A Nubian servant slammed the door behind us, and we took him along, so as to leave no enemy at our rear.

A big, old-fashioned house opened into the garden, and there was no trouble about breaking into that, for the front door stood ajar, and the Nubian who came running from within to ask our business arrived too late. We locked him, the gate-keeper, and the Egyptian who had given the signal that admitted us, into an empty closet at the end of the hall, and charged upstairs with Chu Chi Ying in our midst; he told us that the room where he had told his story was on the first floor.

We made noise enough, of course, to wake the dead, for Tommy Atkins in ammunition boots and armed with a rifle trips on no light fantastic toe; so it was hardly surprising that we found the door that Chu Chi Ying indicated locked on the inside. However, having broken all the laws of Egypt already we did not hesitate to repeat on one of them, and the door went down under the thrust of butts and shoulders.

A strange scene confronted us then. A big, old fashioned sort of drawing-room with red plush furniture, and a plain deal table in the midst. Gilt mirrors everywhere. Eleven Egyptians, most of them with "political" stomachs, rose out of easy chairs and stood looking terrified. Three men at the deal table, one of whom was Zegloush, remained seated, too frightened to move, I think.

"I thought you'd be here presently!" said Joan Angela's voice. "Did you find my bit of handkerchief?"

She and Mrs. Watts were on two small chairs at one end of the room. Their ankles were bound fast to the chair-legs and their hands lashed behind the bent-wood backs. In front of them, on a tray on the floor, was an ordinary woman's curling-iron being heated in an alcohol lamp: why nobody had put that out of sight when they heard us coming is beyond imagination to explain, unless fright paralysed them.

"Oh, hello, Captain Naylor! How nice, meeting you again!"

Her voice was as usual, without a tremor in it. She looked calm, but Mrs. Watts was deadly pale and very nearly fainting. Narayan Singh was first across the room, untying their hands and feet; the rest of us took precautions to prevent a stampede through the door.

"Have they used that hot iron? Have you suffered harm, mem-sahib?" he asked.

She laughed and shook her head.

"I owe you an apology, Narayan Singh," I heard her say.

I couldn't hear what he answered; he growled into his beard, and I was holding by the throat a pasha or a bey or somebody who imagined he could win the door by struggling. Captain Naylor was going the rounds disarming everybody. Three had repeating-pistols, and every single pasha of them had a knuckle-duster; one of them tried his on the British soldier who was holding him, and screamed loudly.

Grim fixed up the door more or less, and stood with his back against it.

"What next, Naylor?" he asked.

"Lord knows!" laughed Naylor, who had got round to where the women were and was resuming the flirtation left off on the steamer. He was a merry-minded little man. "It's up to you, old top."

He walked over to the table.

"What's this?" he asked, picking up a typewritten document.

"That's the title deed they wanted me to sign," said Joan Angela. "I was to be tortured until I signed it, and killed afterward. Did you catch that man who went out? He was on his way to order a cart. The idea was to dump the remains of Mrs. Watts and me in an empty lot some time tonight and blame it on the rioters!"

"Yes, we caught him," answered Grim, beginning to write down the names of prisoners.

They were not asked their names, but identified with indignity from the contents of their pockets, Grim and I witnessing. It was Narayan Singh who thought of what to do next, plucking Grim's sleeve.

"Speak, O man of swift decisions!"

"Sahib, leave me in this room alone with all these!"

"He'd better have help, hadn't he?" suggested Naylor.

Grim nodded, and Joan Angela looked scared.

"D'you mean you're going to kill them all?" she demanded.

"Oh, Lord, no!" answered Naylor.

"Pile your arms outside in the hall, you men!"

The Tommies filed out, grinning hugely. They left their tunics outside, too, and came back rolling up their shirt sleeves.

"Now understand, men," said Naylor. "This is strictly unofficial. Nobody's got to be killed. You've seen ladies put to gross indignity, and you'll govern yourselves accordingly. It's personal between you and these Egyptians. You may fall out for fifteen minutes. Shall the rest of us go outside?" he suggested pleasantly.

So we tiled out, and Narayan Singh reset the broken door in place behind us. We carried all the rifles and tunics downstairs, just as a precaution in case some more than usually active Bey or pasha should contrive to escape through the broken door. Then we went out into the garden to hear music. It was good music, of the sort that Egyptians understand; a little wild for white ears, and without much melody, but with a sort of rhythm to it that was fascinating in its way. Some of the high notes seemed off key, and, in common with nearly an Oriental music, if it possessed harmony it was of a nature unintelligible to the untaught ear. But it fairly pulsed with sounds like drum-beats; that part was comprehensible.

"You see, Joan Angela," said Grim, laughing aloud at a more than ordinarily high falsetto screech that skirled through a broken window-pane, "if we arrested them the secret would be out, whereas if they go and complain about this we've still got perfect evidence against them, and all their names. They're getting thrashed, and that's good for them. They'll be afraid to complain, or to make any further trouble."

"Besides, you know, Miss Leich," said Naylor, "those men of mine put up with no end of dog's work to-day — being hit without hitting back, and all that kind of thing. You wouldn't rob them of an opportunity like this?"

"I'm only sorry Mrs. Aintree isn't in the room. That might make her realize," she answered.

But I did not believe that. I don't believe it yet. She would merely have said that those Egyptians were suffering for their own sins, which of course was true, and would have flattered herself that she was the instrument of Providence.

There began to be more or less silence upstairs-the tune petered out to a frazzled end in fact-before the expiration of the fifteen minutes, so Naylor blew his whistle and the soldiers came down on by one, examining torn shirts, and feeling at bruises. They put on their tunics, picked up their rifles, and fell in in front of Naylor, not grinning, but with the air of men who have put through an important job.

"Now, have any of you helped yourselves?" asked Naylor. "If any man has taken anything, I'll look the other way while he gets rid of it. Looting and justice don't go together, you know."

He turned his back deliberately, but none of them made a move.

"All right," he said. "Fall in then. 'Tshun! Stand at ease! Now, I want no talking about this. If you're asked any questions, refer the questioner to me and answer nothing. You've done a white man's job. It was a great privilege. Now do the right thing by your officer and don't let your tongues get me into trouble. 'Tshun! Back to the lorry now. Forward-march!"

Narayan Singh came last downstairs. He might have been coming from saying his prayers in a temple.

"Such creatures should be skinned and thrown to the crows," he remarked, "but we did the next best thing. What now, sahibs?"

CHAPTER XVI
"Cleopatra, who would have liked to sell Egypt's soul again"

I don't know what the authorities did about Zegloush and his accomplices. Grim took that list of names to headquarters, and we were given permission to go ahead as secretly as possible with the excavation. It is rather easy to guess what happened, however, without shooting wide of the probabilities.

Nothing is more improbable, for instance, than that Zegloush or any of that gang we caught in the upstairs room was in a fit condition to go about for several days. And, as they were not arrested, someone in the confidence of the authorities undoubtedly paid all of them a visit. It is likely that, viper fashion, they showed their fangs and threatened to make public what they knew if they should be prosecuted. Having plenty of trouble on their hands, the authorities preferred to avoid a prosecution, but undoubtedly threatened in return to prosecute and hang the lot if they let so much as a bleat escape them regarding the supposititious Khufu treasure.

Nobody knew exactly, or even nearly, when independence would be granted, if ever, and there was always the possibility that it might come sooner than anticipated; Zegloush stood to gain by keeping the secret. If at the same time he could prevent the existence of treasure from being proved, and keep the treasure underground until after the British let go the reins, there was always a chance that he and his gang might get possession of it. Joan Angela's title to the land would be worth about ten cents if ever Zegloush should be in a position to pull the political wires.

Zegloush and his intimates could still reach channels through which they stirred up the mob, for word of mouth is much more difficult to control than written or printed communications.

So, although we took a gang to Joan Angela's camp, and the authorities quartered an officer and twenty men in the huts for our protection, the neighbouring villagers became more and more threatening, and there even began to be half-veiled hints in the local vernacular press to the effect that foreigners were desecrating ancient monuments and planning to loot the country before the Egyptians themselves could get control.

We weren't out of the wood. Anything at all against any foreigner was good propaganda just at that time. Any violent invective that could arouse the fellahin and set the whole country by the ears was regarded by the would-be statesmen as sound policy. And nothing was more certain than that the first whisper that we had unearthed enormous treasure would plunge the whole country into civil war: for every political party, and almost every individual, to say nothing of the foreign bankers who held Egyptian promises to pay, would stop short of nothing in order to get a share of it.

The solution was the idea of Grim and Chu Chi Yi between them. The engineering end of it was mine. The ticklish work was done by Captain Naylor and the same identical Tommies who had helped Narayan Singh administer "field punishment" that afternoon. Joan Angela paid the expenses, and provided the successful camouflage by granting an interview at the right time to the reporters of several newspapers, including representatives of all the Arabic press, who jeered at her in their columns afterward and mentioned her as "the modern Cleopatra, who would have liked to sell Egypt's soul again, but failed." However, Joan Angela failed in nothing, not even in the fun.

Our task was made at the same time more easy and more difficult by the circumstance that the two members of the council who were in the secret till regarded it as a burlesque. They seemed to think there was perhaps one-tenth of one per cent of a grain of truth underlying our delusion-just about sufficient to set Egypt by the ears, and therefore something to be handled circumspectly. They were all in favour of the trick that Grim proposed to play, but deadly in earnest in insisting that there the whole thing should stop. We had to deceive them, as well as the Egyptians.

The main difficulty was to waste sufficient time, for we needed weeks, not days, to tackle the real job. We had to invent labour trouble, broken derricks, sliding sand and a dozen other expedients to explain why it took so long to uncover the masonry that Atkins had come on when he first began prospecting. We knew that was not the right direction to explore in, but the longer we could keep the rest of the world believing that the treasure was supposed to lie underneath those slabs, the more time we had for real prospecting. So we did things that would have made a striking bricklayer weep for very shame at such loafing and stupidity. Whenever we got enough sand cleared away in order to up-end one of those thirty-ton slabs, either a rope or a chain or a sheer-leg was sure to give way. Or, failing one of those things, all the sand would come sliding down the bank and provide another three or four days' job of digging.

Meanwhile, we pulled down one of the biggest huts and re-erected it on a spot that Chu Chi Ying indicated after making careful measurements; and inside the hut, using a picked gang, in eight-hour shifts, who carried the sand away quite a distance in buckets on their heads, we dug in real earnest. At the end of five days we had uncovered thirty feet of a masonry tunnel that was built as scientifically and substantially as the pyramid itself. We were lucky enough, or else Chu Chi Ying was clever enough with his calculations, to descend on it at a point where it began to curve in order to lead toward the Nile.

During the whole of the time that the digging was going on there was trouble with the near-by villagers, and there was even some talk of reinforcing our small contingent of soldiers, who had to shoot over the heads of raiding-parties sometimes as often as three or four times a day. The shooting was explained in Cairo as "rifle practice."

We had to blast to get into that tunnel we had found. The cement that old Khufu's engineers had used was of such good quality that they had been able to spread it thinner than a sheet of writing-paper, and it had set so that the tunnel was practically one solid piece of stone, forty miles long, without a break or a crack in it anywhere.

Nor was that the least amazing part of it, for it was twenty-one feet deep, inside diameter, and, at the time when we broke in, the upper nine and a half feet were out of water. The rise and fall of the Nile at that point is about sixteen feet, and taking the level of the river at that time into consideration it was obvious that there would always be a considerable air-space all along the tunnel-room, for instance, for a small boat.

So the two chief mysteries now were: Why should Khufu have constructed such an enormous tunnel? and: How had his engineers prevented it from silting up with mud in the course of four thousand years? Even supposing that it flowed in a wide loop and had an outlet back into the Nile at some point lower down, it should have silted none the less, for the Nile carries mud in solution until the water looks like pea-soup, and the mud settles so fast that not only has the whole Nile delta been formed by it, but the river-bed itself is considerably higher than it was in Pharaoh's day.

The first mystery was solved by Grim, who produced some books on ancient Egypt. According to them there was some connection in the Ancient Egyptian mind between dying and going over water-so much so that the funeral processions of wealthy folk were all made in boats. The corpse in its magnificent sarcophagus was taken by boat across a lake, followed by all the mourners.

Apparently Khufu's water journey had been postponed; at any rate no record of it has ever been discovered on any of the walls on which it was customary to depict the personal history of every king from the time of his ascending the throne until his death. Moreover, there was that account given by Herodotus to bear in mind. Herodotus came on the scene more than a thousand years after the event, but according to him the legend in his day was definite that Khufu had been buried in a place unknown, that was connected by a tunnel with the Nile.

So it seemed probable that, in order to avoid too much publicity and the consequent discovery of his tomb by thieves, Khufu had caused the boat-ride to be postponed until after his interment. To a man who could conceive such a gigantic hoax as the construction of the pyramid, with its three million cubic yards of fitted and cemented masonry, it can have hardly called for much additional effort of imagination to consider himself quite capable of taking that ferry-ride alone, without the aid of priests and their assistants. So what could be more plausible than that he should make provision for it by constructing his tunnel high enough for the upper part to be above Nile-level and so leave room for a boat? Whether that guess was right or not, we received some circumstantial confirmation of it later.

It was not long before we solved the other problem, of how the tunnel had been kept clear of mud. But first we had to discover where the intake from the Nile might be, and Chu Chi Ying could give us no pointers about that. He said there were no measurements in the pyramid on which to base calculations for that problem; so we had to go at it from where we were and hunt like rats in a drain.

We procured one of those flat-bottomed duck-punts with a small motor in the stern, in which expensive Egyptians like to fool about among the reeds while their hired men catch ducks in a net. And we blasted and broke the tunnel roof until the hole was big enough to lower the boat through without filling. An acetylene torch and some candles in case the acetylene gave out, four good life-preservers, and some long poles completed the outfit, and we were ready. The boat would hold four without too much crowding, and Joan Angela, Grim, Captain Naylor, and I climbed in. Nothing less than a warrant for her arrest would have kept Joan Angela from coming with us.

We pushed off slowly, using the poles at first, the tunnel echoing to every sound we made, so that we could hardly hear each other speak, and it was by that means that we discovered how the tunnel had been kept free from silt; for the poles went down into a foot or so of mud and then touched rock, except in places. At intervals of about twenty yards there were wide gaps in the floor where the poles went down so deep into the mud that we could hardly pull them out again. The floor on either side of those gaps was at different levels, that farthest away from the Nile being always the higher of the two by at least two feet, and, as far: as we could determine by groping, those were stone pockets whose throats faced the flow of water and caught the silt. The constant repetition of that arrangement for forty miles, and the almost immeasurably slow current, explained why the water reached the well in a condition fit for drinking without being filtered.

We poled perhaps for half a mile before starting up the motor. There was a smell of wet stone, but the air was not too stale to breathe. There was a certain amount of slime on the sides of the tunnel, but that sort of stuff apparently needs daylight to grow rankly, and you could usually see the joints in the masonry, although you couldn't have thrust a knife-blade in between them anywhere.

Crocodiles are supposed to have been exterminated from the lower reaches of the Nile, but not so. There were monsters in there-great, blind brutes whose scales were almost white, and who must have had quantities of fish to live on. There was a ledge a little more than a foot wide along each side of the tunnel about six inches below the present water-level, and the filthy brutes dropped off those ledges in dozens as we sent the rays of the acetylene torch along in front of us. Scales had grown over their eyes, but they were not quite insensitive to light. Their greyness made you think of lepers.

There was no other life down there but crocodiles and the fish, whose presence had to be presumed. Once we got the motor going, and its roar turned the tunnel into the very mother of all noise, we saw not another living thing, but ploughed ahead six miles an hour, leaving a wake behind us that washed the tunnel sides and added its own swishing to the tumult. It was useless trying to speak. Atkins and Chu Chi Ying told us afterward that they could hear the din of our progress until we reached the very end, and that they knew the instant we started back.

There was nothing to mark the distance, and no way of judging it except by time; even so, we did not know the exact speed of the boat and the thought of a collision with submerged rock and an upset among those sightless monsters was no encouragement to us to speed. We throttled the engine down after a while to the slowest rate at which it would keep on turning, and stopped it altogether, using the poles again, whenever we reached a bend-which was about once in every mile or so.

Sometimes there were sharp turns, twice repeated, as if the tunnel engineers had had to avoid tough rock; or they may have been designed as an added precaution against silt. The nearer we approached the Nile, the more frequent those turns were, and the deeper the silt became in the pockets; we lost all sense of direction after a while and, strangely enough, the sensation became one of going down-hill, as if we were descending into the very bowels of the earth, whereas, as a matter of fact, allowing for sand-dunes and ridges, we were at no point more than a hundred feet below the surface.

There is nothing like darkness to make a journey seem interminable, and it felt as if we had been a whole day, instead of six hours, underground when we came to the intake at last, and the tunnel opened out into a vast stone tank, whose roof was made of monoliths, supported on upright pillars eight feet thick that rose out of the water in a long row down the centre.

This was another exhibition of Khufu's royal extravagance; not a stone in that great tank can have weighed less than thirty tons, and some of them-those in the roof particularly-must have weighed two or three hundred tons apiece. And so perfect was the masonry, so accurate the joining and the geometrical design, that not one stone had shifted from its place in all those thousands of years. The place was as perfect as on the day it was built and sealed up.

But it was all right to admire the engineering; what we had to discover was some way of reaching the surface, or at least of identifying the spot, so that we might return and continue operations from above. We could hear the Nile, sucking and swishing and gurgling, but as the intake was under water we could not discover its arrangement, or even guess how Khufu's engineers had solved the problem of silt and rubbish removal at that point. Obviously there was some sort of grating, and it was probably of stone, with spaces wide enough to admit small crocodiles, but too close together to let the grown ones out again. They were certainly wide enough apart to let big fish swim through, else what did the crocodiles eat? But they were invisible; and the bottom just there was fathomless: we drove one pole down so far into the mud that we could not recover it, and nearly upset the duck-punt in the attempt.

It was Joan Angela who thought of the solution. She had been reading about the pyramid, and studying the religions and superstitions of ancient Egypt more than the rest of us.

"If Khufu planned to make his journey after death, along this waterway, how did he propose to escape at this end? He must have left an exit," she said. "Do you recall how, when Al Mahmoun's men forced an entrance into the pyramid, they had almost given up hope when they heard a stone falling in some hollow place inside? There may be some such stone left here that will fall if it gets a shock."

We examined the end of the wall nearest to the Nile, but there was no sign there of any loose stone, or of a stone that could be pried loose with anything less than dynamite.

"Wouldn't he plan to emerge upward?" Joan Angela suggested.

That being probable-for all men seem to think of heaven as being somewhere overhead, although where the Australians and Chinese would go when they die in that case is unpleasant to imagine-we turned the acetylene light on the roof. By standing up in the boat we could very nearly touch the roof with our fingers, so that, as we shifted the boat about and used the torch systematically, we were able to scrutinize every inch of it. Then we saw what we had not seen before-that the middle pillar of all was only two feet thick at the top and was cut in the form of steps all the way down to the water on the side nearest the Nile, at which point it was eight feet thick like all the others. And at about the point where the roof-stones would have rested on that pillar if it had been of the same thickness as the rest, there was a square of limestone set between the granite. It was set flush, and finished off so smoothly that the difference in colour was the only clue to it, and although apparently it was not fastened in place with cement, the joints were so absolutely perfect that friction should have been enough to hold it in place for centuries.

"I'll bet it's dropped in place from overhead, and weighs at least two tons," said Grim without enthusiasm.

"I'll bet!" Joan Angela answered. "Give me that pole. Now, push the boat clear."

She shoved against the stone, but nothing happened, except that the boat shot all over the place and she nearly fell into the water.

"Somebody stronger take a hand," she suggested. So I took the pole, and we shifted the boat so that Grim and Naylor could hold its stern against the next pillar. I shoved so hard that, what with my weight and the pressure, the bow all but went under, and suddenly the limestone moved — not more than a fraction of an inch, but enough to set the end of the wet pole slipping on its smooth surface. I tried to recover my balance, but Grim's hands slipped on the rock he was clinging to and I went overboard at the same instant that the limestone block gave up its four-thousand-year grip on the granite and plunged down into the tank along side me!

I was thinking of hungry crocodiles, and I scrambled out as if the underworld were after me. Above us gaped a four-square black hole, just big enough for one man at a time to pass through Comfortably-King Khufu's gate to heaven!

I went up first and helped Joan Angela through after me. The others followed with the torch and candles. We were in an oblong chamber, thirty feet by twenty, lined with porphyry. There were no beams visible above us, and the porphyry ceiling twenty-eight feet high-as we found out afterwards-glowed as smoothly as the hand-rubbed floor and walls. It was a piece of absolutely perfect workmanship, and empty. There was not even dust, and the air was almost impossible to breathe.

But at one end, that nearest the Nile-the eastern end that is-there was a perfect Egyptian doorway in the middle of the wall. It was apparently a blind door, for the space between the marvellously moulded uprights was filled up with the same smooth porphyry that covered walls, floor and ceiling.

We could not stay then to examine it; we were gasping for air already, and although a little air came in through the square hole we had entered by it would only have been a matter of seconds before we all collapsed. So we climbed back into the boat, Joan Angela first, and I last. I lingered to make sure of the direction of that door.

"There must be an earth-mound overhead," I said. "We can find that from the outside. Joan Angela, we've won the game! Old Khufu pays the bets!"

CHAPTER XVII
Magnificent simplicity

It was after midnight when we emerged from that tunnel and found Chu Chi Ying and Atkins waiting for us. They had had some trouble in keeping inquisitive labourers at bay, but having heard our engine barking in the tunnel all the while had only been in doubt about our safety when we stopped the thing. According to Atkins they could not distinguish a word we said, but could identify our voices miles away.

Chu Chi Ying's face wrinkled into smiles as he sat listening to us, nodding like an automatic toy.

"Sometime finding porphyly chamber same size, same shape, same evlything upstairs in pylamid," he announced with an air of conviction. "Way out pyramid top-side. Find him some day. Me savvy."

He was really only interested in the pyramid. The treasure did not attract him; what gave him exquisite delight was seeing the proof that his deductions were correct. He was too old to care for money, or too wise; I don't know which. Our motive from now on became wholly mercenary.

Dawn found us down by the Nile in two Ford cars, exploring for a mound to correspond with the porphyry chamber and the tunnel's end. We found it. There was a place where a great grey rock thrust itself a short way out into the Nile and rose for fifty feet above the water. Inland, its southern end was all rock, but it shelved downward toward the north and north east, and there the earth had lodged so deeply that a fellah saw fit to own it, rig up a water-wheel, and grow crops. Joan Angela bought that piece of land from him at his own price—a price that would have put a war-crazed alien profiteer to shame; and he went away disappointed and grumbling at having been robbed, with a fortune in his pocket.

Then we really went to work; but first we had to build a long shed for camouflage, and in doing that we unearthed the stone foundations of an ancient temple. There was nothing whatever remaining of that old temple except foundations, part of the flooring, and one end wall with an unroofed chamber behind the wall that had been used by the priests for their mysteries. You find the same sort of chamber in all old Egyptian temples, but the remarkable part about this one was that it backed against the rock, which had been trimmed off vertically and carved to represent doorposts. The space between the doorposts was blocked with one enormous granite slab whose edges were so beautifully mortised into the carved post as to be almost undiscoverable without a magnifying glass.

We had to get ropes and lumber on the scene before we dared tackle that granite slab and, even so, we had to chip the edges with a chisel all the way round before we could insert a wedge to pry it loose-only to discover then, to our amazement, that it was no false door, nor yet a covering set in place to conceal a door, but the actual door itself. It was balanced in the middle, top and bottom, and revolved on stone hinges when a pressure of about a hundred pounds was applied to the right-hand side.

It gave access to a narrow passage in the rock of about: twice its own width. That passage was twenty feet long, and blind, but the end of it was built of porphyry, and when we set a jack against a plank up-ended on the porphyry wall and began to apply pressure exactly the same thing happened; a porphyry door revolved against the clock, away from us, and we walked straight through into that marvellous, empty, polished chamber above the tank at the secret tunnel's end.

Now Khufu and his priests no doubt intended that marvellous piece of architecture to symbolize the awe-inspiring emptiness and peace that await all royal applicants at heaven's gate. But the floor was good and slippery, and we danced on it. I would just as soon play golf or tiddly-winks as dance, but Joan Angela insisted, so we did the U.S. two-step all over Khufu's floor. Maybe we'd better say that she did, and I did my best. Grim and Naylor did a breakdown, South Carolina style, though Naylor refused to tell where he learned that noble art. We had solved how to get the treasure out without betraying it, providing there was treasure! Counting your chickens before they are hatched is profitable business, despite the proverb-mongers, if you do it in the right mood.

Nothing remained to do at that end, except to keep intruders away. The next thing was to build a dam across the tunnel, at the point where we originally blasted our way in, and then pump the water away from Khufu's island tomb, which we were confident of reaching by way of the well as soon as all the water was exhausted.

But that was a lengthy job. We had to get cement to start with, and set up forms, and mix and pour the stuff, observing without much pride the difference in quality between our cement and the mixture made by Khufu's engineers. The job had to be done carefully, because if the dam should give way, enough water could come flowing down that tunnel to drown us all in a very few minutes.

We procured a good American rotary pump from a dealer in second-hand machinery, and an oil-fired steam-engine to drive it. You can get any kind of black man to wet-nurse a boiler, but what the same man can do to a kerosene- or gas-engine would take two skilled mechanics to adjust again.

There was no trouble, of course, about getting rid of the water. We simply pumped it out over the dam and back into the tunnel toward the Nile; but there were hours, and even days, when we suspected we had merely cut a circular tunnel in the middle and were trying to pump the whole Nile not only dry but back into itself. An immense space had to be cleared of water-not only the lake surrounding Khufu's tomb, but galleries and holes and tunnels, whose purpose none has guessed yet, but whose aggregate content was prodigious.

We finally got a second pump and another engine, and the two together gave us a twelve-inch flow of water, which began to make an impression. Meanwhile, we had to keep on working at the false excavation, and long before the pumping was finished the sand was thrown so far back, and so many of the huge monoliths were exposed that we could invent no further excuse for delay. So we got a new, stout sheer-legs set in place, with a hoisting gear capable of lifting thirty tons, and after another day's hard labour contrived to get a chain round one of the stones. All we could do then was to hoist the monolith and set baulks of timber under it, which was enough, though, to provide access to the gloom below.

And oh, the rush when the baulks were in place at last and the great stone came to rest on them! Every hired man on the lot, Tommies and Gyppies and all, went down through the dark slot like rats into a hole, imagining gold and diamonds and all the farms and public-houses and motor-cars the loot would buy! They did not wait for lamps or candles, but probably expected to find their way by the light of the gleaming gems that would be heaped up in piles in the tomb. And at that, they were no bigger fools than the rest of us, who buy gilt-edged stock in mines that don't exist.

We were in no hurry. Chu Chi Ying was much too positive and had hitherto been much too often right in his calculations for us to buy any stock in that hole; so we sat on top and waited for reports, merely sending down a lantern by the last man-a private from the Tower Hamlets of London Town. We waited for an hour, listening to the rumble of their voices and the occasional sound of great stones being shifted, before the same man showed his face in the opening once more, lantern in hand.

"Gawd blimey, it's a dormitory!" he remarked.

"A perishin' vault full O' lines O' drinkin'-troughs, wi' lids on 'em what weighs a ton apiece! Inside, nothing but blokes' bones, what all died kickin'! Come an' see, miss!"

"No treasure?" she asked.

"Not a thripenny bit. And we've 'unted!"

We climbed into a spacious vault that looked as if it had been hewn from solid rock, but was patched up with masonry in places to make it rectilinear and smooth. It was three hundred feet long from end to end, and down the length of each side, in triple rows, were plain stone sarcophagi, from most of which the lids had already been forced by our gang of invaders-a simple enough business, because they had not been fastened down in any way, but had been kept in place by sheer dead-weight.

There were no wooden coffins inside those stone boxes; no mummy- wrappings, nor any of the usual trappings of the Egyptian corpse; but inside each was a grown man's skeleton. Not one of the lot lay straight. The legs of some were raised, as if they had died in the effort to force off the stone lid. They had been buried naked and alive. And what was worse, some gruesome stuff had been put in with them, to preserve them.

We had the gang lift off every lid, and with the aid of lamps and candles we examined each interior carefully. There was not in any one of them the slightest trace of ornament or jewellery, or of anything that could identify the individual or explain the reason for his burial alive. But Chu Chi Ying laughed. A Chinaman can always see humour in cruelty; even the best of them seem to have that characteristic.

"Damn fools bury Khufu. By an' by priests bury them. Dead men not say much!" he remarked. That was the long and short of it. Those were the bodies of men who carried Khufu into his last resting-place, treasure and all, and the priests had stopped their mouths-unkindly, as the way of such priests is.

Well, we had a story for the newspapers, at any rate. We had an alibi, and perfect proof of the failure of our excavations. We had a story for the soldiers and the labour-gang to tell in barracks and bazaars, and something to show the reporters, who came out and grinned at Joan Angela. We stopped the pumps, that afternoon of the famous interview that all the papers published with such scathing sneers at "foreign Americans, who think they know so much, but whose brains are nothing better than mechanical, producing no literature worthy of the name," so nobody got wise to the fact that we had other excavations under way.

A very learned Egyptian professor burst into print with the explanation that the place we had found was an execution dungeon for the worst type of criminals, and neither very ancient nor of more than casual interest. A discovery has to be "hig-liff" and distinctly more than casual to interest Egypt. Even the fellahin began to be less troublesome.

So we were able to cut down our guard of British Tommies to the original ten under Naylor's command, hand-picked by him; and with them we made a bargain, which, as far as I know, every single man has loyally kept. That done, and the last inquisitive reporter gone to write his acridly sarcastic comments, we resumed work with the pumps, while Grim went back to Cairo to confer with the financial member of the council and arrange for a Government boat to lie at anchor close by our new shed on the bank of the Nile.

It was a peculiar coincidence, which nobody ever seemed to notice, that that gas-driven, white-painted, yacht-lined inspection-boat was manned and occupied exclusively by officers, who lay aboard and yawned, and wondered at intervals what the confounded tamasha was all about. But they were young men, who had been told, although by no means everything, too much to care to ask for further information.

One thing that we did while waiting for that water to disappear was to pull down several of the wooden huts belonging to the camp and saw them up into short lengths ready to be nailed together in the form of rough boxes. It might have given the game away if we had ordered boxes made in Cairo.

There came a day at last when the pumps sucked little else but mud, and choked accordingly. By that time we had a wooden shed built over the well, with a door that could be barricaded from the inside as well as padlocked from without; and inside that hut we had high rubber boots, lanterns, electric torches, picks, crowbars, and two of those ever useful screw-jacks with which you can shift almost anything that can be shifted. We also had a stout beam fixed in place across the top of the well, from which a rope-ladder hung, and we had plenty of rope in addition for making safe our further descent into the unknown labyrinths.

The hut had no windows, and two of our Tommies guarded the place on the outside. We even had food with us, to avoid the necessity for interrupting our explorations. We started the descent so provided in every way that we could find that treasure, and get rid of it too, if expedient, without once coming to the surface.

Joan Angela claimed the right to go down first, and after some argument we let her have her way, that being the only possible solution, for she would not yield. So down she went with a lantern in hand, and I went next after her, armed with a club. The rope-ladder was easy, of course, but nothing could have been more difficult than that slippery ramp below, down which I had nearly drowned myself on the first prospecting trip. Even with a good stout rope to cling to, it was impossible to keep your feet, for the slime of centuries had established itself on the smooth stone, and our descent became a series of spasmodic efforts to check the speed. Somewhere up above us Mrs. Watts let go the rope and screamed; Naylor tried to get in her way by throwing his legs out, but she carried him with her, and the two dropped down on top of me, one on each side of me, clinging to each other; it was the sheerest piece of luck that I did not let go the rope and lower the lot of us down on top of Joan, in which case there would have been four first-class casualties for a beginning.

For from the lower lip of the descending ramp, that connected the well with the underground cavern, to the floor of the cavern itself was a drop of more than forty feet. We had to go down hand-over-hand, swinging in darkness, and, as I said, Joan Angela went first; but she surrendered her lantern to me, and by holding to the rope with one hand I contrived to attach the lantern-bail to the end of a ball of twine and to lower it foot by foot as she descended.

Mrs. Watts was in a hopeless predicament, for she was afraid to go over that edge, yet unable to get back. Nobody wanted to go down ahead of her, for fear she would let go her hold and fall on the unfortunates below. So finally, after a lot of talk, and after Joan Angela had called up cheerily to me to let go the lantern because she stood on rock bottom, I took Mrs. Watts down pick-a-back, as the only way out of the difficulty-and a darned, difficult, knuckle-breaking, desperate expedient at that!

Then, standing at the bottom, peering about us by quivering lantern-light, we got another illustration of Khufu's forethought. He had conceived it possible that someone in the centuries to come might empty out the water by some means, and had made provision for their reception after they should lose their footing on the slippery ramp and come hurtling downward. The rock on to which we had to step as we let go the rope was carved into regularly spaced fangs three feet in height, two feet or so apart, and of about the same shape and thickness as an elephant's tusk. It would have been absolutely sure death to fall on them. Nor was that all. There were crocodiles-blind, white-scaled monsters in there-waiting to finish what the stone fangs left undone! My instinct that day when I made the first descent was right.

Joan Angela screamed and jumped. I brought down my club on a brute's snout in the nick of time. If they couldn't see, they could smell or else hear, and nine of them came slithering their tails to left and right across the slimy floor, their teeth rattling like castanets and their great claws scratching on the rock.

There was no swarming up that rope again to safety, for the others were coming down it. The only chance was to stand among those stone fangs and use the club until Naylor could get down with his Army revolver. Naylor had only six cartridges. The blind brutes set their snouts and armoured claws between the stone uprights, and tried to force their shoulders through to reach our legs, and if you think they did not fight back when their snouts were struck you have another guess due. They hissed, foaming at the mouth, and although they could not see, as we speak of sight, whenever I struck at one of them another was certain to snap at the club, and several times my arm was within an ace of being caught in the clattering jaws.

And stink! It was worse than carrion, that smell of the guardians of Khufu's tomb, much worse. Carrion is stuff you can understand; the reek of those filthy reptiles told of centuries of unintelligible gruesomeness.

When Naylor got down he put six shots into them, and five took effect; but that left four of the monsters to be dispatched by some other means, and although crocodiles are not nearly as dangerous out of the water as when in it, in spite of superstition to the contrary, one medium-size wooden club was no argument. Moreover, something had to be done about it fairly soon, for the soldiers were swarming down hand-over-hand behind us, and there was not going to be room for all of us to stand between those fangs of rock. On the other hand, lantern-light seemed to have some effect on their scale-covered eyes, for they rushed at the lanterns, so that whoever stepped outside that pale had either to fight in the dark or else expose himself to double risk.

The ultimate solution was clumsy, but effectual. We had to put all lights out except one, and swing that on outward on a pole that one of the soldiers had brought along for exploration purposes. The brutes snapped and hissed at that, and I swatted them. I'm a hefty specimen, and what I hit most usually breaks, but it was rather too much of a cave-man shambles to come under the heading of amusement.

Then, though, at last we were ready for the great adventure, and it was merely a matter of minutes then before we knew the secret of Khufu's burial arrangements, although that was not the whole of the problem yet.

Herodotus was right. Chu Chi Ying was right. We were in a cavern of vast dimensions that entirely surrounded an island of rock. And the rock under the island was undermined, so that it stood on rows of rectangular stone uprights, and when the cavern was full there was water over, under, and all around it. On the floor of the basin between the island and the outer walls there were no less than twelve deep pits with sloping sides, presumably for catching silt, which they had done, whether or not that was their purpose, for they were all about two thirds full.

We walked all round the island without discovering any means of entry, but it had been so obviously trimmed off square by hand, and was so plainly artificial at one corner, where masonry had been added to bring it into alignment, that the mere absence of an obvious opening did not discourage anybody, We made the circuit three more times, like the children of Israel parading round Jericho, but no walls fell for our convenience, although quite a lot of optimism dawned.

For one thing, there was the strength of those stone uprights to be considered. They were beautifully shaped, and arranged rather like the whalebone in a "right" whale's mouth; and each one in itself was slender when compared to the bulk of the island overhead. Each was much too small, for instance, for a man to have burrowed upward through it to avoid the water; but there was a veritable forest of them, spaced hardly more than a foot apart, and they were obviously intended to bear a prodigious weight-something heavier than the island itself, which could have been supported safely by less than a quarter of their number. That gave us ground for believing that the island was hollow, and that the hollowness had weight enclosed in it.

The soldiers favoured blasting. That was just the military point of view, which is certainly practical enough in an age when the walls of cities no longer fall conveniently at the prayer of invading hosts. But there was something a lot too dignified, and stately, and calmly beautiful about the proportions of that wonderful island for the rest of us to care to use dynamite without trying other means first. Even Chu Chi Ying, a convinced iconoclast, who cared for nothing under heaven but the calculus and its solution, and who had come down the rope on Grim's back because he said it was time to die soon, anyhow, so that danger did not matter time any more, was indignant at the suggestion of shooting away the props until the whole mass should collapse. Moreover, the dynamite was up aloft in the shed beside the well, and nobody wanted to shin up there and fetch it.

So we got the soldiers to make a platform of their backs, and clambered up on to a ledge that faced toward the eastward at the island's narrowest end. From that point of vantage the ledge seemed like a threshold and the island like a small dark temple of beautiful proportions, perfect in design and measurements as the Great Pyramid itself. In length, it was about a hundred and twenty feet; in breadth, sixty; in height, perhaps twenty-eight; but there were no doors or windows visible, nor any indications of a door, so we had the wooden pole passed up and used it on the wall in front of us in the same way that Koreans ring their great bells. The wall boomed hollow!

"If his body is inside there, I'll bet you Khufu left some way of getting out without too much exertion," said Joan Angela, "Try pushing hard."

But I had another intuition of impending danger. I took the pole first, and did some measuring. Making a rough estimate-for the pole was too short for accuracy —I came to the conclusion that if there was a door in the wall that faced us, and supposing it were made out of one huge slab, that slab would be long enough when lowered to form a ramp from the threshold to the floor of the cavern. Supposing such a stone to be lowered in that way, it would make a fairly convenient means of sliding up heavy weights, such as a stone sarcophagus, and if unwelcome intruders were to be standing on that threshold when it should fall outward...

"And on whomsoever it falls, it shall grind him to powder," I said. "Suppose we all get off here!"

So we did. There was no means of setting a screw-jack against the perpendicular stone, for the threshold sloped downward at an angle of thirty-five degrees, and if my surmise was correct, that the facing rock was hinged at the bottom, a jack set against the lower end would not have done much good. The problem was how to get that great slab to fall forward, supposing that it really was designed to do so, and at the same time, how not to be underneath it when it fell.

The surface was absolutely smooth. There was not a crack to be seen, although that could partly be accounted for by the deposit of dark slime. The only way that I could see out of the difficulty was to damage some of the supports after all, on the theory that the weight on the floor might then cause a fractional sag, which would tilt the door forward and start it.

But there we were faced by another difficulty, for those uprights were so closely set together that nobody could force his way between them; and to stand in front to do the damage would mean the imminent risk of being crushed under the falling door. It began to look as if someone would have to go back for the dynamite, but I decided to try one forlorn expedient first.

So we set to work with the picks and crowbars, and tried to smash the uprights at either corner, not expecting to produce a sag in the floor so easily as all that, but hoping that the vibration of the blows might communicate itself through the masonry and loosen something above that depended on balance for its stability.

And about the tenth blow turned the trick! A section of stone in the middle of the front wall, amounting to a fifth of the whole width, tilted outward from the top without warning and fell with a two-hundred ton crash, so that it broke loose from its stone hinges below and smashed itself to fragments on the cavern floor! The din was an explosion. The cracking stone sent splinters whizzing like sharpened shrapnel.

But some of the broken pieces were large enough to form stepping-stones, and we scrambled up, flashing our lights into the gap the monolith had left. But our lights fell on another blank wall, of polished granite this time, and again I had an idea to call our party back. No amount of striking at the supports seemed to make any impression on that sheet of polished granite, so I tried poking at it with the pole from as far to one side as could be managed, so as to avoid the thing if it fell on me. But instead of falling outward like the other, it showed symptoms of revolving on a central hinge, yielding an appreciable fraction of an inch when I thrust against the pole with all my might.

"Let's all get up there now and shove," suggested Naylor.

But I still had an idea. It seemed to me that a man who had thought of that simple means of flattening intruders, by balancing a monolith to fall forward on them, might also have thought of something slightly more intricate by way of a trap for such fortunates as had escaped the falling door. It would be the most natural thing in the world to get up there and shove against that polished granite the moment it showed signs of yielding. If Zegloush Pasha had been with us, or even Moustapha and Mrs. Aintree, I would have sent them up to shove without an atom of compunction. I know others, too, whom I might have employed without prejudice on that occasion. But the gang we had with us was a good gang, and Joan Angela is simply irreplaceable.

I sat down for a minute to think, and the sharp edges of the broken stone I sat on hurt the part that I sit with and provided the idea. That piece of stone weighed about two hundred pounds and it occurred to me that if we could catapult it in some way against the granite leaf, that might be hint enough for any hidden mechanism to start performing.

We had plenty of rope and a good, stout pole, but you need rather more than that to construct a working catapult in fifteen minutes. However. I had the idea all right and a pendulum is just as good. There were two sockets high up in the sides of the opening into which stone projections had fitted to help preserve the balance of the outer monolith. I cut the pole to an exact length to fit across the opening with one end in each socket, and stood on the shoulders of Grim and Atkins while I fitted the pole in place; it had to be forced in, and made a good, tight fit.

The rest was simple. All we had to do was to throw the rope over that beam, tie the rock to one end of it, and haul up until we could set it swinging at the proper level. In that way we were able to deliver blows on the granite leaf that amounted to something.

I guess we swung the rock against the granite knocking on Khufu's bedroom door for admittance, as you might say, nine or ten times before anything happened. Then, however, the granite revolved at least a foot. And then the top fell free from the retaining socket, and the whole mass tumbled outward, as the first had done. I don't think it weighed more than ten tons; but ten tons are enough.

That was the last of Khufu's hints to strangers. The tomb yawned wide, and we climbed up over the debris to investigate, Joan Angela leading the way with an electric torch. And the first sight was bitter disappointment —disillusion-anticlimax-although beautiful; you had to admit that it was beautiful.

There was only a narrow passage down the midst of the rock, and at the end of it one plain sarcophagus of hand-rubbed granite, resting on a carved stone boat. Khufu had even provided the ship in which he proposed to sail to heaven down that forty-mile-long tunnel he had made! That was all there was in there. That sarcophagus did not hold wealth enough to settle the debts of nations.

Yet, as I said, it was beautiful, for the tomb had been watertight. Not even damp had entered to spoil the gilding. All down one side, the wall was finished in dull gold; in silver all down the other, although the floor and ceiling were of polished granite and there was no skirting-board or decoration of any kind to conceal the joint between granite and gold and silver; it struck me that it would have looked better if there had been something of the sort.

However, we all hurried along to the sarcophagus, and got busy with crowbars prying off the lid-no easy task, for the lid weighed tons, rested in a mortise, and was fastened down with stone pegs that were difficult to find. However, we got it off at last, and tipped it over sideways against the gold wall, where it knocked off a section of solid gold sheeting about six feet high by three in width, for all the world like a piece of wall-board, and of about the same thickness, but heavy enough, of course, to fall like lead; and it had the ring about it that no man ever mistakes for anything but gold when he has heard it once.

Joan Angela screamed, not with fright but with sheer amazement. There was no more gilt in that place than there was garlic! The walls on either hand were lined with solid gold and silver sheets supported on granite uprights, and behind them on either hand the gold and silver treasure of Khufu was stacked in ingots from floor to roof, rows and rows and countless rows of them without a fraction of an inch between except where passages were left that gave just enough room for a broad-shouldered man to pass!

All was gold on one side. All was silver on the other, and whoever could estimate the value of it all has quicker brains than I have. Even Chu Chi Ying refused to state the amount approximately; he sat down on the boat that bore Khufu's sarcophagus, with a "told you so" expression on his face, and borrowed a cigarette from Grim. I take it that was his comment on the situation.

The simplicity was magnificent. There was no attempt at ornament, inscription, comment, explanation. There lay Khufu, and there was his money-or rather the money he had wrung and raked and filched from Egypt in the course of fifty years. Inside the stone sarcophagus was the customary wooden one, and another wooden one inside that again, but never a mark or hieroglyph on any of them to announce who the occupant might be.

We raised the inner lid of all, and there lay his mummy, plainly wrapped, with the jars containing entrails alongside of him; but we did not pull the wrapping off the mummy, for it seemed a shame to risk damaging the relics of that arch old miser, who could live so masterfully thoughtful for his latter end and die in such prodigious state.

Consider the gall of the old rascal! Think of wringing all that bullion in taxes from the folk who had to build the pyramid to help him hide the place where he proposed to stow it all away! And then consider him lying there without so much as a name on his coffin, but with all that good money to right and left with which to purchase his way into heaven-and within a hundred yards of him the dungeon in which the men who had stacked the bullion were done to death!

And what hold had he over the priests, do you suppose, that prevented them from telling the next king where Egypt's treasure lay? The next man must have come to a throne whose treasury was empty, and although the priests of those days took small stock in kings, but rather used them as an adjunct to the priestly power, you would think they would have made some use of their secret knowledge. For they must have known of that treasure. Nothing could be done in those days without the knowledge of the priests, nor even without their permission. Wouldn't the story of the politics of that make better reading than the quarrels of the League of Nations?

However, our job, like Khufu's, was accomplished. There remained no more to do than to set a guard over the tomb, and to start that prodigious treasure on its way in the duck-punt along that forty-mile tunnel to the Government boat that waited near our big shed by the Nile. The bargain we lad made with the soldiers was that they should hold their tongues and be paid, provided sufficient treasure were discovered, the equivalent of five thousand pounds apiece. Naylor received his reward from the authorities direct, and I don't know how much it amounted to; but Joan Angela refused to touch a nickel's worth of the treasure, subject to her one original condition, that the British should appoint trustees to use the treasure in the public interest, and that she herself should be one trustee.

And, of course, neither Grim nor I could take any of it, for we were the employees of a firm that had undertaken a definite task for a stipulated fee, to include expenses. Joan Angela paid Meldrum Strange's bill in due course, and that ended our connection with the affair.

But if you want to check me upon this story, I will point to a few clues that you may follow if you wish.

In the first place, then: There are ten ex-private soldiers who all purchased their discharge from the British Army on the same date, and who are all now settled in business in one English county town. That's only a coincidence, you might say, but here's another one: On Joan Angela's ranch in California there is a man named Atkins who is boss storekeeper, and generally responsible for goods and chattels. He seems to have private means, for he drives his own car, and smokes cigars of a kind that you and I can't afford much oftener than once a year.

And here's yet one more clue: In Singapore, in a little side street that runs down toward the quays, there lives a Chinaman named Chu Chi Ying, who teaches no more "fat-fool first mates" how to pass examinations for their master's ticket, but smiles nearly all day long and amuses himself by making marvellous astronomical calculations. He seems to have an income quite sufficient for his needs, and a portrait of Joan Angela hangs on the wall just inside the doorway of his house. Go and look, if you don't believe me. On your way, consider the stuffed, blind, white crocodile in the Gezivich Museum, Cairo.

And finally, there's this: have you heard of the Khufu Trust Fund? There are very few who have not heard of it-almost equally few who know exactly what it does, although there are a hundred thousand rumours and certainly not less than a million schemes afoot to loot it. Perhaps you are even one of the hopeful who have tried to get your fingers in the pie?

I have been promised that before long I may tell the story of the Fund. I believe it will rather surprise you to learn how more intelligent rogues than old Khufu, and how even the armour barons failed to levy tribute from it.

After all, old Khufu had proposed to himself to spend that money in the next world. Nobody knows, at any rate yet, what the next world is.

If that should be a too exciting hint, try to bridle your impatience and imagination until the trustees keep their promise to let me be the first to tell the use that has been made of Khufu's money.

THE END

Printed in Great Britain
by Amazon